Energy Psychology
Theory, Research, & Treatment

Journal of the National Institute for Integrative Healthcare (NIIH.org)

www.EnergyPsychologyJournal.org

Energy Psychology: Theory, Research, and Treatment is a peer-reviewed professional journal dedicated to reporting developments in the field of energy psychology (EP) that are of interest to health care professionals and researchers. It contains original empirical research into the efficacy of EP methods; theoretical, experimental and basic science papers illuminating the mechanisms of action of EP; clinical insights on the application of EP to various populations, and interfaces with other interventions; book reviews, and abstracts published in other journals that are of relevance to the EP field. Its goal is to further the development of EP as an evidence-based method in the healing sciences. It conforms to the editorial, stylistic, and ethical standards of the American Psychological Association (APA.org).

Energy Psychology: Theory, Research, and Treatment (ISSN 1949-6575) is published bi-annually (November and May) by Energy Psychology Press, PO Box 442, Fulton, CA 95439. For customer service or advertising information contact 707-237-6951 or energypsychologypress@gmail.com.

POSTMASTER: Send address changes to: *Energy Psychology* journal, PO Box 442, Fulton, CA 95439.

YEARLY SUBSCRIPTION RATES: $49.95 per issue, $99.95 per year.

AUTHOR ENQUIRIES: Submit paper copies of proposed papers to *Energy Psychology* journal, PO Box 442, Fulton, CA 95439. Include an email address and phone number for the corresponding author. All submissions should conform fully to the requirements of the *Publication Manual of the American Psychological Association,* sixth edition. Include a cover letter as specified on the "Submissions" link at www.EnergyPsychologyJournal.org, and manuscripts should be prepared in conformity with the other standards published there. Acceptance or rejection will be made via email; paper copies will not be returned. If a submission is accepted for peer review, all subsequent contact will occur via email. Deadline for Spring issue submissions is Jan 15 of each year, and July 15 for Fall issue.

REPRINTS: Back issues are available for $49.95. Reprint ordering information may be found at www.EnergyPsychologyPress.com. To order 100 or more copies of a particular paper, contact energypsychologypress@gmail.com.

www.EnergyPsychologyJournal.org

Contents

May 2014 • Volume 6, Number 1

About

ENERGY PSYCHOLOGY: THEORY, RESEARCH, AND TREATMENT

Energy psychology (EP) is an evolving and maturing field that is rapidly meeting the standards of proof for "evidence-based" practice. Studies of EP have demonstrated its efficacy for a wide range of psychological and physical problems, from phobias to pain to posttraumatic stress disorder. EP is now being researched in hospital systems such as Britain's National Health Service (NHS), large private hospital chains such as Kaiser Permanente and Sutter Health, and the United States Department of Veterans Affairs (VA). By providing a rigorous, high-quality, peer-reviewed platform for the publication of research results, theory, and clinical insights, this journal provides a forum for the exchange of the key discoveries and ideas that drive the EP field forward.

—Dawson Church, PhD
Editor, *Energy Psychology: Theory, Research, and Treatment*

The journal publishes work in the following areas:

EDITORIAL ESSAYS include guest editorials from some of the best thinkers and researchers in EP today;

ORIGINAL RESEARCH provides empirical evidence for various EP methods;

CLINICAL REPORTS describe the use of EP with challenging conditions and specific populations and provide guidance for empirical research;

INTERFACES WITH OTHER THERAPIES show how EP is typically used in conjunction with other methods, such as cognitive behavior therapy (CBT), mindfulness therapy, addiction counseling, sports psychology, medicine, energy medicine, meditation, and life coaching;

REVIEW ARTICLES are theoretical papers, literature reviews, reports of innovations, and analyses that explore issues from the professional condition of EP to the physiological mechanisms of action of EP;

BOOK REVIEWS cover new and classic EP-related titles;

ABSTRACTS published in other journals relevant to EP are reprinted.

EDITORIAL BOARD

EDITORIAL ESSAY

The Translational Gap: How the Medical System Obstructs Effective Patient Care

Dawson Church

There is something deeply flawed about the modern scientific enterprise. As a result of this problem, millions of people suffer unnecessarily. This phenomenon prevents advances in medicine and psychology from flowing quickly and efficiently from laboratory to clinical practice. This lag between scientific discovery, and the translation of those discoveries into clinical practice, is called the "translational gap."

How large is the translational gap? Around the turn of the century, the U.S. Congress commissioned the Institute of Medicine to find out. It published a report in 2001 (Committee on Quality of Health Care in America, 2001). The institute found that it takes 17 years for innovations to travel from laboratory to patient. Only 30% of innovations jump the translational gap; the benefits of the remaining 70% are lost to society. Essentially, patients are receiving only 30% of emerging therapies, and they're getting them 17 years late. The report characterized the size of the translational gap as a "chasm."

Given the demand for high-quality medical and psychological care, and the obvious benefit to patients and to society, what force is capable of blocking progress so effectively?

There are several factors that contribute to creating the translational gap. A primary one is the suspicion and even ridicule to which new discoveries are subject. Established therapies have large followings and institutional support. New therapies do not. Followers of established therapies attack new ones as they emerge. With the weight of evidence behind an old therapy, and very little evidence for a new therapy, it is easy to contrast the two. These attacks have a chilling effect on the development of promising new therapies.

Second, the way funds are allocated by private and public grant-making agencies discourages innovation. A recent case in point is the U.S. federal government's new PCORI program. The Patient-Centered Outcomes Research Institute was supposed to foster patient-centered care. I recently participated in a PCORI application prepared by the California Pacific Medical Center (CPMC), a well-respected research facility. The application was for a novel smartphone-based depression treatment. It was turned down on narrow technical grounds. PCORI went on to fund highly academic endeavors such as discovering whether receiving assistance filling out assessments affected the responses geriatric patients gave, and measuring the difference between individuals within randomized controlled trials and the average results obtained. The PCORI failed to fund exploration of potential benefits to patients of a smartphone-based depression treatment.

The same lack of support for innovation is evident in the peer-review process as well. Little or no attention is given to the strengths of a paper, while the deficiencies, real or supposed, are mercilessly scrutinized. Carl Rogers called this process "finding the blemish." Even after a paper passes the peer-review gamut and is published, critics often pick it apart, finding some trivial methodological characteristic with which they disagree and then dismissing the results entirely. The baby is thrown out with the bathwater, and promising new treatments are discredited before they can develop.

Third, institutional gatekeepers often exclude therapies with which they are unfamiliar. A case in point is the online list of "empirically validated treatments" maintained by Division 12 of the American Psychological Association. According to the website (http://www.div12.org/PsychologicalTreatments/faq.html), the purpose of an online list is to allow "regular updates." For certain therapies, the list is indeed regularly updated, but for others it is not. Studies of Cognitive Behavioral Therapy and Acceptance and Commitment Therapy dating from 2012 are posted on the website (http://www.div12.org/PsychologicalTreatments/treatments/anxietymixed_act.html). By way of contrast, the list of studies of EMDR has not been updated for 15 years (http://www.div12.org/Psychological-Treatments/treatments/ptsd_emdr.html). The Division 12 criteria for what constitutes an "empirically validated treatment" provide objective standards by which a therapeutic method can be judged (Chambless & Hollon, 1998). Yet rather than leveling the playing field between old and new therapies, the selective reporting espoused by the editors of the website presents a picture of effective therapies skewed by their preferences.

The Division 12 criteria are in themselves very useful. They define seven characteristics that must be present in a study in order for it to validate a treatment method. These characteristics include such reasonable practices as randomization, statistical significance, and the use of a treatment manual. For a technique to be regarded as "efficacious" it must be validated in two such studies conducted by independent research teams. The U.S. Food and Drug Administration (FDA), considering the criteria for drug trials at the same time as the Division 12 standards were being developed, also adopted the standard of two randomized controlled trials (Food and Drug Administration, 1998). When the Division 12 standards were defined in the late 1990s, an initial online list of "empirically validated" therapies was published. That the list has since been updated selectively is unfortunate but is no reflection on the original standards. Standards are essential, even when they are not impartially applied.

Some sources go much further in discouraging the development of novel treatments. A group of self-appointed "skeptics" has appropriated the editing of the Wikipedia entries on alternative medicine. They are organized as Wikiproject Skepticism, and they specialize in vandalizing entries on topics they hold in disfavor. These include acupuncture, chiropractic, energy medicine, and energy psychology. The entry for EFT (Emotional Freedom Techniques) excludes mention of the more than 50 studies and review papers evaluating the technique. Instead it uses old newspaper stories debunking the method, quotes from highly partial sources such as Quackwatch and the Skeptical Enquirer, and reviews critical of EFT. To make sure that readers get the point, the entry as of February 2014 used the word "pseudoscience" three times in its five-paragraph length. The page is locked to outside edits (most Wikipedia entries are open for anyone to edit) and the administrating editors have resisted all attempts to change the entry to a neutral point of view.

Having new breakthroughs accepted is an old problem. Medical history is replete with examples of the translational gap. In 1847, Ignaz Semmelweis discovered that if doctors washed their hands between the morgue and the operating room, infections dropped by 90%. His modest reforms were robustly opposed, and after he was driven out of his job, his successor reversed his handwashing policy.

The cure for scurvy was discovered in 1747, but the British Admiralty did not start routinely issuing citrus fruit to sailors for another 42 years. In that time frame, Britain fought the American War of Independence, the Napoleonic Wars, and many other conflicts. It desperately needed sailors to maintain its global fleet, but failed to take action on this simple remedy. More sailors died of scurvy than from the guns of all the navies that Britain fought. All the exigencies of national security, public health, and global trade could not overcome the translational gap.

These battles between old ideas and new ones are cloaked in the language of scientific discourse, but they are more like religious or political arguments. If you've attempted to reason with a fundamentalist, you quickly realize that when you trespass into the realm of devout belief, rational argument is futile. The mind of the fundamentalist is firmly set, and any facts must fit into that conceptual scheme, or be discarded. The 19th century battle between the theory of evolution and the biblical account of creation was one of the more famous landmark arguments of this type. Another was the battle between Galileo and the Catholic Church over whether the sun revolved around the earth or vice versa.

I admire the skeptics in the same way I admire all people of faith. They have a strong belief that they are right, and they are immune to reason. In the "talk" pages of Wikipedia, where you can read the debates behind the entry on EFT, one of the gatekeepers controlling the content discusses "the best way to demonstrate to the reader that this is bullsh*t!" (http://en.wikipedia.org/wiki/Talk:Emotional_Freedom_Techniques/Archives/2011/May). Their line of thinking goes like this: Energy psychology is bunk; therefore any evidence that it is not must be incorrect.

When you start with this dogma, it becomes necessary to explain away any scientific fact that contradicts your fundamental belief. The creationists faced precisely this dilemma in the 18th and

19th centuries when Britain's system of canals was being dug. The excavations unearthed fossils of extinct species and revealed strata of rock from past epochs. These made it apparent that the age of the earth was much greater than the one suggested by a literal reading of Genesis. One fossil can be explained away. The task becomes harder when more are discovered, and impossible once a coherent theory such as evolution offers a new and more reasonable explanatory paradigm through which to view the evidence.

The skeptics find themselves in this same difficult position, and I admire the tenacity with which they cling to their beliefs. At first there were clinical reports of the efficacy of energy psychology, and these were dismissed by the skeptics as "merely anecdotal." Then there were hundreds, and then thousands of case studies. The skeptics retorted that "the plural of anecdote is not data." Then there were data. The first studies were published. The skeptics shifted their ground, now arguing that there were not enough studies. More studies were published. The skeptics moved the goal posts again, arguing that these used "shoddy methodology" or had other flaws that required them to be dismissed. Higher quality and independent studies then validated the early studies and the anecdotes.

The reason I admire the skeptics is that it takes strong faith to dismiss a mountain of evidence, just as creationists today still dismiss the theory of evolution. I personally do not have such strong faith; when I see the mountain, I am convinced.

Not all new approaches have merit. Some are passionately promoted by adherents, and later turn out to be flawed. From "phrenology" in the 19th century to "conversion therapy" in the 20th, the history of science is littered with concepts that did not stand the test of time. Yet if we don't subject new therapies to microscopic scrutiny, isn't there a danger that quackery, fraud, and even dangerous techniques will flourish?

This is where standards like those of APA's Division 12 and the FDA show themselves to be essential. A therapy must meet such standards in order to cross the threshold of acceptability. The requirement that a method must be validated in not just one randomized controlled trial, but a second one conducted by an independent research team, is a practical standard of proof. At that point, it's possible to proceed with reasonable confidence.

If the battles between old and new approaches were merely an academic debate, it would be amusing. When it results in a translational gap that prevents effective treatments from reaching millions of suffering people, it is a tragedy.

Former Intel CEO Andy Grove has written stinging critiques of the failure of medicine to innovate. He contrasts this with the world of technology, in which innovation is constant. He describes a medical culture that creates "conformity of thoughts and values," which leads to "more sameness and less innovation." (Begley, 2007). Imagine if medicine and psychology innovated as enthusiastically as smartphone manufacturers.

This issue of *Energy Psychology* journal is devoted to exploring some of the problems that lead to the translational gap. It includes two papers that were denied publication in other journals. Those papers were written in response to reviews critical of energy psychology. When the editors of those journals received cogent rebuttals of their reviews, they refused to publish them. We include abstracts of the original reviews, and those authors' responses to the rebuttals. Read both points of view, and decide for yourself whether or not these approaches have merit.

We also feature a guest editorial by Robert Schwarz, PsyD, director of the Association for Comprehensive Energy Psychology, an organization which has given professionals in the field a collective voice.

It's not likely that we will quickly close the translational gap. The old enemies of knowledge—ignorance, fear, superstition, arrogance, intolerance, complacency, and entrenched elites—are alive and well. Almost a century ago, physicist Max Planck famously observed that "Science advances one funeral at a time."

However, the speed with which online journals can publish research means that new disciplines such as epigenetics and psychoneuroimmunology can be advanced quickly. Despite the opposition, EFT is now practiced in many VA (Veterans Administration) hospitals. Over 40% of professionals are using energy psychology with their clients (Gaudiano, Brown, & Miller, 2012). Millions of Google searches are performed each month for terms like "EFT therapy," and millions of people visit EFT websites each month (Church, 2013). As the technologies championed by Andy Grove meet the translational gap embedded in modern medical superstition, our prospects of getting effective evidence-based practices to the people who need them most may improve markedly in the coming years.

References

Begley, S. (2007, November 3). A research revolution. *Newsweek*. Retrieved from http://www.thedailybeast.com/newsweek/2007/11/03/a-research-revolution.html

Chambless, D., & Hollon, S. D. (1998). Defining empirically supported therapies. *Journal of Consulting and Clinical Psychology, 66*, 7–18.

Committee on Quality of Health Care in America, Institute of Medicine. (2001). *Crossing the quality chasm: A new health system for the 21st century*. Washington, DC: National Academy Press.

Food and Drug Administration. (1998). *Guidance for industry: Providing clinical evidence of effectiveness for human drug and biological products*. Rockville, MD: U.S. Department of Health and Human Services.

Gaudiano, B. A., Brown, L. A., & Miller, I. W. (2012). Tapping their patients' problems away? Characteristics of psychotherapists using energy meridian techniques. *Research on Social Work Practice, 22*, 647–655. doi:10.1177/1049731512448468.

Deconstructing the Six Anti-Scientific Strategies for Denying a Highly Effective Therapy (Energy Psychology)

Robert Schwarz, Association for Comprehensive Energy Psychology, Ardmore, PA

Abstract

This editorial describes a pattern of six basic interlocking and antiscientific strategies of discourse used by writers and editors who are deeply biased against energy psychology despite evidence in favor of its efficacy. These strategies attempt to obscure their positions under a patina of objective evaluation. The level of distortion has reached new heights in the recent publication of two highly biased and inflammatory articles (Gaudiano, Brown, & Miller, 2012; Bakker, 2013) followed by the refusal of the editors of each journal to publish responses written by well-qualified experts in the field. In this way, antagonistic assessments of the energy psychology field are presented as objective reviews, while scientific discourse is stifled. The goal of this editorial is to cast light on this process of distortion, so that clinicians, consumers and policymakers can better evaluate the evidence for the efficacy of energy psychology.

Keywords: Energy Psychology, Thought Field Therapy, Emotional Freedom Techniques, censorship, bias

Robert Schwarz, PsyD, DCEP, is a clinical psychologist and Executive Director of the Association for Comprehensive Energy Psychology. **Correspondence:** 233 East Lancaster Ave, Suite 104, Ardmore, PA 19003. Email: drbobschwarz@mac.com. **Disclosure:** The author receives income from professional activities relevant to the approach discussed.

I was invited to write this editorial after two incidents of quasi-censorship occurred in separate journals following attempts to counter articles attacking the efficacy of energy psychology (EP) practices and the integrity and gullibility of EP's proponents. In 2012, *Research on Social Work Practice* published a highly biased and inflammatory article by Gaudiano, Brown, and Miller (2012). Sise, Leskowitz, Stein, and Tranguch (2014) asked the journal's editor, Bruce Thyer, to consider a rebuttal. He invited them to submit one and described plans to have Gaudiano et al. and others comment on the rebuttal. Once the rebuttal was written, it was not published in the journal. The rationale Thyer provided for this change, of course, was simply that he disagreed with the rebuttal, which was not surprising, as he had allowed the severely slanted Gaudiano et al. article to be published initially.

In 2013, *Clinical Psychologist* (an Australian journal) published a highly biased article by Bakker (2013). This time Feinstein (2014) submitted a rebuttal. His rebuttal was turned down after a peer reviewer who had published one of the most disdainful pieces about EP ever to appear in a journal (Devilly, 2005) reviewed it unfavorably, claiming that it was Feinstein who was biased.

As both rebuttals are published in this issue, readers can review them and decide for themselves their scholarship and value. I am not going to repeat their arguments here. My goal in this editorial is to deconstruct the antiscientific tactics used by those attempting to discredit EP while claiming the scientific high ground. The stance and tone taken by anti-EP commentators have ranged from vicious accusations that EP supporters are snake-oil salesmen motivated only by money to charges that EP is pseudoscience without any research to condescending denunciations of the gullibility and poor reasoning abilities of clinicians who use the method.

The pertinent issues are further confounded because clinicians and researchers have very different mindsets and use very different criteria for evaluating the effectiveness of treatment methods.

Each position has benefits and problems that I do not assess here. EP is part of the cutting edge of psychotherapeutic treatment that has been focusing on the body, or below the neck approaches (e.g., Levine, 1997; Porges, 2013; Siegel, 2007, 2010). Therapeutic use of EP has grown so much because clinicians have found it to be more effective than talking alone and other above-the-neck approaches.

Those of us who research or write academically take these clinical findings and generate more scientifically rigorous data, a developmental process that is common in scientific research. Furthermore, those of us who focus on larger systems see these clinical findings and research data and want them to be used to solve societal problems. Perhaps the most salient current example is posttraumatic stress disorder (PTSD) in veterans. There is enough evidence to suggest that EP approaches *could be* a major advance in addressing this epidemic that has been overwhelming the capacities of the mental health community. Compared with the amount of money spent on wars that are hurting our young men and women, only a modest investment would be needed to research finding out whether EP methods are as good as the advocates of EP believe them to be. As Feinstein points out in this issue (p. 35):

> A monograph by the Institute of Medicine of the National Academy of Science—*Crossing the Quality Chasm: A New Health System for the 21st Century*—reported that "an average of about 17 years is required for new knowledge generated by randomized controlled trials to be incorporated into practice" (Committee on Quality of Health Care in America, Institute of Medicine, 2001, p. 13).

While this 17-year delay may be typical, it is not desirable that thousands of people suffering with a serious disorder are not receiving what may well be the best treatment available. What I and many others advocate is that EP, which has now been investigated thoroughly, be recognized as a legitimate PTSD treatment, allowing our soldiers, veterans, and citizens suffering with PTSD and other serious disorders get the most effective treatment available. The speed and efficacy of EP treatments would make them highly cost-effective, which should entice the U.S. Department of Veterans Affairs or Department of Defense to fund a large clinical trial to further investigate these approaches.

One factor inhibiting the translation of EP into wide practice has been the vehemently negative reviews by a small number of academic writers. I want to focus on the process that is often obscured under the patina of an allegedly objective evaluation. There are six basic interlocking strategies used by those who want to mount an offensive against EP. These strategies are deeply antiscientific. They are essentially tactics used in political discourse to win adherents to one's side.

Strategy 1: Write "Reviews of the Current Literature" That Ignore All or Most of the Current Literature That Supports Energy Psychology

In the vernacular, do not let the facts get in the way of your story. Both Gaudiano et al. (2012) and Bakker (2013) leave out large swaths of research data published in scientific journals. Bakker's article is particularly egregious, as its title is *"The Current Status of Energy Psychology: Extraordinary Claims With Less Than Ordinary Evidence."*

There have been at least 17 studies on EP published in peer-reviewed journals from 2008 to 2013. Six of these studies were published in *Energy Psychology: Theory, Research and Treatment*, seven were published in a variety of other journals, and four were published in what are generally considered top-tier journals, such as *Journal of Nervous and Mental Disease.* Bakker (2013) included 12 of 17 studies in the reference section. However, in the body of the article he actually discussed only 2 of the 17 published studies. Furthermore, instead of summarizing the findings according to the original authors, he devoted most of the article to describing the methodological flaws of the studies.

Gaudiano et al. (2012) used a fantastical slight-of-hand trick, stating the following:

> A recent review of the literature concluded that EMTs (energy meridian tapping) lack a valid scientific basis, show nonspecific efficacy, are not superior to other treatments, and display multiple characteristics of pseudoscience (Devilly, 2005). (Gaudiano, p. 649).

Devilly (2005) is one of the gospels of the anti-EP forces that is always cited (see Strategy 2).

It is anything but a "review of the literature" or "recent." Gaudiano et al. (2012) cited 0 of 17 (since 2008) additional published articles on EMT. With their false premise in hand, they then made the following biased and distorted proposition for the entire study.

> Nevertheless, EMTs remain popular and many therapists appear interested in learning the techniques despite the disconfirming studies presented by researchers and therapists. Therefore, an important question remains: Who is using EMTs? (p. 649).

Gaudiano and Bakker also ignored the fact that the 50 or so peer-reviewed publications on EP are almost unanimous in supporting it as an efficacious treatment. What is particularly disturbing is that under the guise of supporting the scientific process, these authors attacked EP as being nonscientific—yet they ignore the first rule of the scientific process: Look at the data. In this issue, Bakker (2014) stands truth on its head when he claims "support for energy psychology's efficacy has flat-lined" (p. 44). Feinstein (2014) counts the studies and demonstrates that the support not only is not flat-lining, it is accelerating.

Strategy 2: While Engaging in Strategy 1, Continue to Cite the Same Few Articles Again and Again That Support the Anti-EP Proposition Even Though They Are Outdated, Disputed, and Mostly Commentary

The articles in question are Devilly (2005), Herbert and Gaudiano (2000), Lilienfeld (2007), Pignotti (2005), Pignotti and Thyer (2009), and Waite and Holder (2003). If you look at anti-EP articles, these citations are almost always used. Disputations of these articles, however, are never cited. If you compare the publication dates of anti-EP to pro-EP publications (see Sise et al., 2014, p. 21), you will notice that the number of publications in EP are, as I just mentioned, accelerating. In fact, it is the anti-EP publications that have flat-lined.

In this issue Bakker (2014) leans heavily on Waite and Holder (2003) in their attack on EP. Although he makes some legitimate points, he frames the data in all-or-nothing terms (part of Strategy 3 below) and jumps to conclusions not supported by the facts. Bakker suggests that Waite and Holder was a knock-out blow that invalidated all of the EP data, which is not accurate. The second of the two so-called "negative" studies (Pignotti, 2005) does not disconfirm EP in any major fashion. Pignotti only demonstrated that one aspect of Thought Field Therapy (voice technology) is not particularly more effective than random tapping on acupuncture points. Her study showed that virtually everyone got better when meridian points were tapped regardless of the sequence. It hardly invalidates the entire field.

It is significant that in the past 12 years there have not been any data that can be interpreted as being disconfirming other than Waite and Holder or Pignotti (2005). If EP is a bogus therapy, why are no disconfirming data appearing? Why are the confirming data becoming more plentiful?

Strategy 3: Never Give Partial Credit; Always Frame the Discourse in All or Nothing Terms; Refuse to Frame the Issue in Any Developmental Fashion and Do Not Accommodate Any New Evidence From Any Other Field of Endeavor Even If Relevant

When you read Gaudiano et al. (2012), Bakker (2013, 2014), or other articles cited in Strategy 2, and compare them to Sise et al. (2014) or Feinstein (2010, 2012, 2014) you will rapidly note massive differences in editorial tone. The latter noted various advances in the methodologies of outcome studies as well as other advances in other fields, while commenting on various needs for improvement. The former suggested that no advances have occurred; nor have their been any methodological improvements in EP studies, such as control groups, effect size, and follow up—which is not accurate.

Sise et al. (2014) and Feinstein (2014) explicitly acknowledge that there are many questions still to be answered, and there is a lot more research to do. Ironically, Gaudiano et al. (2012) and Bakker (2013) pointed out the excesses in the early years of EP, something that Sise et al. and Feinstein (2012, 2014) explicitly acknowledged. In fact, the EP community has taken the lack of scientific study criticism to heart and has been accelerating the growth and methodological quality of research over the past 10 years. Gaudiano et al. (2012) and Bakker (2013) could be taken more seriously if they gave credit to the gains that have been made in EP research and then suggested various methodological improvements to increase the scientific rigor of future studies.

Strategy 4: Make Ad Hominem Attacks on Supporters of EP

This is done in two ways. First, say that the author is biased, because he or she has some financial interest in the approach. This attack has mostly been leveled at Feinstein's (2008, 2010, 2012) reviews of the literature. This approach is problematic on many levels. First, Feinstein followed the rules of the American Psychological Association and other journal publishers in acknowledging these potential conflicts of interest.

Second, the argument is specious. It assumes that financial matters do not influence every aspect of scientific endeavors. This is the opposite of the truth. Currently, scientists must spend a large part of their time getting grants that pay their salaries. So they have embedded financial interests in successful research and making sure that the way they conduct their scientific efforts will be deemed by the powers that be as grant worthy. This occurs across the board, and it deeply affects the scientific method. Are the anti-EP forces also saying that all research supported by drug companies should be dismissed? To level this charge on one person who happens to take a different stance is absurd.

Third, and more important, their approach hides a deeper and potentially more significant bias, namely professional ego. Gaudiano et al. (2012) repeated the charge of financial conflict of interest, but they then declared that they have "no potential conflicts of interest with respect to the research, authorship, and/or publication of this article" (p. 653).

In fact, Gaudiano has a significant *potential* conflict of interest. He has already published highly critical articles on EP, for example, the Herbert and Gaudiano (2000) article that has been routinely cited by people in this camp. It should also be noted that the editor of *Research on Social Work Practice*, who first said he would publish Sise et al.'s article in the journal and then decided against it once it was submitted, is Bruce Thyer. This is the same Bruce Thyer who coauthored the highly critical article on EP (Pignotti and Thyer, 2009).

Unfortunately, Gaudiano et al. (2012) have taken ad hominem attacks to a new level with their so-called research into the so-called personality characteristics of the therapists who use EP techniques. They erroneously interpreted their findings to suggest that therapists who use EP suffer from insufficient critical thinking abilities. In this issue, Sise et al. do a superlative job of debunking the seriously flawed arguments in Gaudiano et al., although they are far kinder than I am about to write. If sufficiently critical thinking had been employed rather than personal bias and emotion, Gaudiano et al.'s article would never have been written in the first place, or if it had been written, it would not have been published in its current form.

Strategy 5: When in Doubt Frame Any Positive Findings in the EP-Related Literature as Placebo

Better yet, frame EP as somehow having a "super placebo" effect (Bakker, 2013, p. 3). It is perfectly necessary and reasonable to want to account for placebo effects. The scientific method creates experiments that constrict the amount of extraneous variability. Nonspecific placebo effects with human subjects are a group of variables that are well known and typically can account for up to 30% of healing or positive outcome. A classic example of this was in knee reconstruction surgery. Subjects either had real knee reconstruction or fake reconstruction. The same percentage of subjects in both samples got better! (Moseley et al., 2002).

The term *super placebo* is an oxymoron. To discount EP because it has "extraordinary placebo effects" is nonsensical. When you describe something as having super placebo qualities you are admitting that there is more going on than regular placebo. That means it is not placebo anymore—by definition.

Strategy 6: Focus the Argument Heavily on the Underlying Energy-Oriented Theories About the Energy-Based Mechanism of Action That Have, to Date, Been Difficult to Substantiate

There are several problems with this stance. First, it takes the position that since the mechanism of action cannot be pinpointed to energy systems, such as meridians, the approach is invalidated and is even pseudoscientific. This argument is in error on several levels. A quick review of the *Physician's Desk Reference* for medication reveals that, in many circumstances, the mechanism of action of a drug is not clear (PDR, 2013). This does not stop physicians from prescribing. The fact that a phenomenon cannot be easily measured does not disqualify scientific discourse. It can take decades and billions of dollars for physicists to create the means to test and measure their theories. It has only been in the past decade that scientists could measure the positive effects of meditation on the brain. Does that mean that meditation has not been effective for the previous 2,000 years?

The EP critics have completely ignored the theory and data in the EP literature that suggests that EP methods may influence therapeutic change by interacting with commonly accepted concepts in neuroscience, such as regulation of affect through the amygdala. In his comments in this issue, Bakker continues to make the point that any benefit obtained by EP is due to known effects such as exposure. What is the point of this argument? It has long been acknowledged in the EP literature that Emotional Freedom Techniques (EFT), Thought Field Therapy (TFT), and other approaches are at least partially based on exposure. One would think that the psychotherapy community would welcome the efforts of EP clinicians and researchers to tie EP into existing psychological principles. Instead, they take the stand that "there is nothing new here, so what is all the fuss about." Research, on the other hand, suggests that stimulation of acupoints adds power to cognitive behavioral therapy (CBT; Zhang, Feng, Xie, Xu, & Chen, 2011) and that stimulating the meridian system is an active ingredient (Fox & Malinowski, 2013; Wells, Polglase, Andrews, Carrington, & Baker, 2003; Zhang et al., 2011).

The question regarding the mechanisms of action in EP is absolutely intriguing. There certainly are legitimate questions regarding whether the purported meridian-based energy system has a decisive role in EP approaches. For that matter, when looking at the common patterns in highly active therapies like Eye Movement Desensitization and Reprocessing (EMDR) and EP, I have raised the question that it might not be the actual procedure of tapping or bilateral stimulation that provides the therapeutic benefit. It might be the larger common metapattern used in these approaches (Schwarz, 2012). As a clinician-scientist, I find these questions fascinating. An answer that passes the scientific methods' criteria is not yet available; however, this does not mean that these approaches do not work.

Research as well as a torrent of reports from clinicians shows that they do work. This line of questioning might mean that more than one approach works. It might mean that there is a final common pathway of all these approaches. The work of Ecker, Ticic, and Hulley (2012) included interesting possibilities. They suggested that any therapy that changes how memory is reconsolidated may be effective.

Historically, the rallying claim for the detractors of EP has been that they are trying to protect the public from snake oil therapists peddling placebo remedies to the naive. This position has continued to appear in their publications, even with little evidence to support it. An alternative position, sometimes simultaneously but implausibly held by the same individuals, is that EP is simply using the same principles as other therapies such as CBT, so while it is effective, it should not be considered a legitimate therapy.

More important, it may in fact be that EP is more effective than other therapies. When a research study on the use of EFT for treating posttraumatic stress disorder in veterans (Church et al., 2013) has been almost twice as effective in half the time of the more accepted approaches of CBT, cognitive processing, and exposure (Bryant et al., 2008; Monson et al., 2006), why is there not more curiosity? The potential stakes include saving billions of dollars and improving hundreds of thousands of lives. This is certainly grounds for urgent study followed by rapid dissemination if it holds up to high research standards.

Conclusion

I am aware that if people have a strong opinion on one side of this debate or the other, their minds are not likely to be swayed by anything I have said. My focus is on communicating to those in the middle: mental health providers, gatekeepers, and consumers or policy makers, who might not be intimately involved with the details of EP methods or research. It is not easy to parse the different perspectives and make informed decisions. I refer readers to the articles in question. Read them and judge for yourselves on the specific merits of each point. As you read these articles and the original articles (not in this issue) to which they refer, look for the six antiscientific patterns of persuasion used by anti-EP forces that I have described and factor them into your judgment.

References

Bakker, G. M. (2013). The current status of energy psychology: Extraordinary claims with less than ordinary evidence. *Clinical Psychologist, 17*(3), 91–99. doi:10.1111/cp.12020

Bakker, G. M. (2014). A bigger swamp is still a swamp: Comments on Feinstein (2014). *Energy Psychology: Theory, Research, and Treatment, 6*, 44–47.

Bryant, R. A., Felmingham, K., Kemp, A., Das, P., Hughes, G., Pedutoa, A., & Williams, L. (2008). Amygdala and ventral anterior cingulate activation predicts treatment response to cognitive behaviour therapy for post-traumatic stress disorder. *Psychological Medicine, 38*, 555–561.

Church, D., Hawk, C., Brooks, A. J., Toukolehto, O., Wren, M., Dinter, I., & Stein, P. (2013) Psychological trauma symptom improvement in veterans using EFT (Emotional Freedom Techniques): A randomized controlled trial. *Journal of Nervous and Mental Disease, 201*, 153–160.

Committee on Quality of Health Care in America, Institute of Medicine. (2001). *Crossing the quality chasm: A new health system for the 21st century.* Washington, DC: National Academy Press.

Devilly, G. J. (2005). Power Therapies and possible threats to the science of psychology and psychiatry. *Australian and New Zealand Journal of Psychiatry, 39*, 437–445.

Ecker, B., Ticic, R., & Hulley, L. (2012). *Unlocking the emotional brain: Eliminating symptoms at their roots using memory reconsolidation.* New York, NY: Taylor & Francis.

Feinstein, D. (2008). Energy psychology: A review of the preliminary evidence. *Psychotherapy: Theory, Research, Practice, Training, 45*, 199–213.

Feinstein, D. (2010). Rapid treatment of PTSD: Why psychological exposure with acupoint tapping may be effective. *Psychotherapy: Theory, Research, Practice, Training, 47*, 385–402.

Feinstein, D. (2012). Acupoint stimulation in treating psychological disorders: Evidence of efficacy. *Review of General Psychology, 16*, 364–380. doi:10.1037/a0028602

Feinstein, D. (2014). Comment on "The current status of energy psychology": Growing evidence for extraordinary claims. *Energy Psychology: Theory, Research, and Treatment, 6*, 35–43.

Fox, L. (2013). Is acupoint tapping an active ingredient or an inert placebo in Emotional Freedom Techniques (EFT)? A randomized controlled dismantling study. *Energy Psychology: Theory, Research, and Treatment, 5*(2), 15–28.

Gaudiano, B. A., Brown, L. A., & Miller, I. W. (2012). Tapping their patients' problems away? Characteristics of psychotherapists using energy meridian techniques. *Research on Social Work Practice, 22*, 647–655. doi:10.1177/1049731512448468

Herbert, J. D. & Gaudiano, B. A. (2005). Moving from empirically supported treatment lists to practice guidelines in psychotherapy: The role of the placebo concept. *Journal of Clinical Psychology, 61*(7), 893–908.

Levine, P. (1997). *Waking the tiger: Healing trauma—The innate capacity to transform overwhelming experiences.* Berkeley, CA: North Atlantic.

Lilienfeld, S. O. (2007). Psychological treatments that cause harm. *Perspectives on Psychological Science, 2*(1), 53–70.

Lilienfeld, S. O. (1998). Pseudoscience in contemporary clinical psychology: What it is and what we can do about it. *Clinical Psychologist, 51*(4), 3–9.

Monson, C. M., Schnurr, P. P., Resick, P. A., Friedman, M. J., Young-Xu, Y., & Stevens, S. P. (2006). Cognitive processing therapy for veterans with military-related posttraumatic stress disorder. *Journal of Consulting and Clinical Psychology, 74*, 898–907. doi.org/10.1037/0022-006X.74.5.898

Moseley, J. B., O'Malley, K., Petersen, N. J., Menke, T. J., Brody, B. A., Kuykendall, D. H., ... & Wray, N. P. (2002). A controlled trial of arthroscopic surgery for osteoarthritis of the knee. *New England Journal of Medicine, 347*(2), 81–88.

PDR Staff (2013). *Physicians Desk Reference.* Montvale, NJ: PDR Network.

Pignotti, M. (2005). Thought Field Therapy voice technology vs. random meridian point sequences: A single-blind controlled experiment. *Scientific Review of Mental Health Practice, 4*, 72–81.

Pignotti, M. & Thyer, B. (2009). Some comments on "Energy psychology: A review of the evidence": Premature conclusions based on incomplete evidence? *Psychotherapy, 6*(2), 257–261.

Porges, S. (2013). *The Polyvagal theory: Neurophysiological foundations of emotions, attachment, communication, and self-regulation.* New York, NY: Norton.

Schwarz, R. (2012). Enhancing traditional therapy with energy psychology interventions. *National Psychologist, 22*(2), 7.

Siegel, D. (2007). *The mindful brain: Reflection and attunement in the cultivation of well-being.* New York, NY: Norton.

Siegel, D. (2010). *Mindsight: The new science of personal transformation.* New York, NY: Bantam Books.

Sise, M., Leskowitz, E., Stein, P., & Tranguch, A. (2014). Critical thinking in the energy therapies: Comments on Gaudiano et al. (2012). *Energy Psychology: Theory, Research, and Treatment, 6*, 21–32.

Waite, W. L. & Holder, M. D. (2003). Assessment of the Emotional Freedom Technique: An alternative treatment for fear. *Scientific Review of Mental Health Practice, 2*, 20–26.

Wells, S., Polglase, K., Andrews, H. B., Carrington, P., & Baker, A. H. (2003). Evaluation of a meridian-based intervention, Emotional Freedom Techniques (EFT), for reducing specific phobias of small animals. *Journal of Clinical Psychology, 59*, 943–966. doi:10.1002/jclp.10189

Zhang, Y., Feng, B., Xie, J. P., Xu, F. Z., & Chen, J. (2011). Clinical study on treatment of the earthquake-caused post-traumatic stress disorder by cognitive-behavior therapy and acupoint stimulation. *Journal of Traditional Chinese Medicine, 31*, 60–63. doi:10.1016/S0254- 6272(11)60014–9

ORIGINAL ABSTRACT

Reference: Gaudiano, B. A., Brown, L. A., & Miller, I. W. (2012). Tapping their patients' problems away? Characteristics of psychotherapists using energy meridian techniques. *Research on Social Work Practice, 22*, 647–655. doi:10.1177/1049731512448468

Objective: The objective was to learn about the characteristics of psychotherapists who use energy meridian techniques (EMTs). **Methods:** We conducted an Internet-based survey of the practices and attitudes of licensed psychotherapists. **Results:** Of 149 survey respondents (21.4% social workers), 42.3% reported that they frequently use or are inclined to use EMTs. EMT therapists reported higher use of a number of techniques from different theoretical orientations, reliance on intuition in decision making, positive attitudes toward complementary and alternative treatments, erroneous health beliefs, and importance placed on the intuitive appeal of evidence-based treatments. EMT therapists also had lower scores on a test of critical thinking. **Conclusions:** Results suggest that a number of characteristics differentiate therapists who are inclined to use EMTs, which can aid in future educational efforts.

REVIEW ARTICLE

Critical Thinking in the Energy Therapies: Comments on Gaudiano et al. (2012)

Mary Sise, Private Practice, Albany, NY, USA
Eric Leskowitz, Harvard Medical School, Department of Psychiatry, Boston, MA, USA
Phyllis K. Stein, Washington University School of Medicine, Division of Cardiology, St. Louis, MO, USA
Anthony Tranguch, Columbia University College of Physicians and Surgeons, Department of Psychiatry, New York, NY, USA

Abstract

Gaudiano, Brown, and Miller (2012) report that of 149 licensed psychotherapists who responded to an Internet-based survey, 42.3% said that they frequently use or are inclined to use Energy Meridian Techniques (EMTs). Gaudiano et al. portray EMTs as lacking an empirical basis and displaying multiple characteristics of pseudoscience. They conclude that EMT therapists may be characterized as relying on intuition in decision-making, holding erroneous health beliefs, and showing lower scores on a test of critical thinking. This reply by clinicians who use EMTs demonstrates that, contrary to the claims of Gaudiano et al., there is a substantial body of research supporting the efficacy of EMTs, that theories underlying EMTs have an empirical basis, and that an affinity toward EMTs is not incompatible with critical thinking abilities.

Keywords: energy psychology, critical thinking, evidence-based practice, Thought Field Therapy, Emotional Freedom Techniques

Correspondence: Mary Sise, 596 New Loudon Road, Latham, NY 12110, USA. Email: marysise100@gmail.com; Tel: 518-785-8576; Fax: 518-783-4793. **Author Note:** Comments on earlier drafts of this paper by Daniel J. Benor, MD, Dawson Church, PhD, David Feinstein, PhD, Philip H. Friedman, PhD, Philippe Isler, MA, Robert Pasahow, PhD, and Meghan Sise, MD, are gratefully acknowledged. **Declaration of Conflicting Interests:** The authors write, teach, and/or provide clinical services on the topic of this article. **Funding:** The authors received no financial support for the research, authorship, and/or publication of this article.

Energy Meridian Techniques (EMTs) are at the core of a novel family of physical and psychological therapies that work with acupuncture points and associated energy pathways known as meridians (Stux & Hammerschlag, 2001). When applied to psychological problems, specific acupuncture points are stimulated, usually by tapping on them, while a targeted memory or trigger is brought to mind. This combination is believed to send electrochemical signals to the brain that reduce elevated limbic activity, alleviating a range of psychological symptoms (Church & Brooks, 2010; Mollon, 2007b). Best known through the practices of Thought Field Therapy (TFT) and Emotional Freedom Techniques (EFT), these psychologically oriented EMTs also include other approaches that fall within a class of treatments called "energy psychology." EMTs, and energy psychology in particular, have been controversial (e.g., Lohr, 2001; McNally, 2001; Pignotti & Thyer, 2009), with Gaudiano, Brown, and Miller (2012) contending that they lack efficacy and credible mechanisms of action, and also that they are beset by flawed thinking among their proponents. This paper is a response to those concerns.

Early EMT practitioners claimed strong, rapid outcomes with disorders that are difficult to treat, including posttraumatic stress disorder (PTSD), prior to the availability of published efficacy research. With the mechanisms of action for the approach also being elusive, they pointed to formulations from ancient healing traditions or hypothesized constructs such as "thought fields" (Callahan & Callahan, 1996) rather than relying on established psychological principles in accounting for the efficacy they were claiming. The skepticism generated by these bold assertions and unconventional explanations is reflected in the difficulty the American Psychological Association had in deciding whether to allow its continuing education (CE) providers to offer psychologists CE credit for energy psychology courses. It required more than a dozen years to lift its initial 1999 ban (Murray, 1999), despite mounting evidence for the effectiveness of the approach. Within the context of this struggle for a fair assessment, the paper by Gaudiano et al. is of particular concern. In an apparent attempt to invalidate EMTs, whose popularity in clinical settings is on the rise, the authors fail to accurately cite the accumulating research support and assert that EMTs "lack a scientific basis" and "display multiple characteristics of pseudoscience" (p. 649). They also characterize those who utilize these methods as being more likely than other clinicians to promote erroneous health beliefs and to have an aversion to critical thinking.

Gaudiano et al. go even further, recommending that therapists using EMTs undergo additional training and education to help them overcome their "affinity toward controversial therapies" (p. 653). They, in fact, call for "future research to investigate whether targeting individual factors related to [this affinity] can improve therapists' critical thinking skills and the use of evidence-based practices." They suggest that training programs should address the "personal and emotional draw and appeal of EMTs" (p. 653), a conversion therapy of sorts. The educational workshops they propose would teach therapists "to better differentiate scientific from pseudoscientific claims" (p. 653). Therapists should, after all, "not only be trained in what to use but what not to use" (p. 653). We fully agree that sound clinical judgment and the ability to distinguish effective from ineffective interventions are both required of competent psychotherapists. However, the authors' *a priori* judgments, clear from the onset, run counter to growing scientific evidence, which they neglect to acknowledge or cite in their article.

Each of the authors of this rebuttal to Gaudiano et al. uses EMTs and holds a decidedly different perspective from the one presented in the Gaudiano paper, "Tapping their Patients' Problems Away? Characteristics of Psychotherapists Using Energy Meridian Techniques." In this response, we challenge the claims of Gaudiano et al. that EMTs fall within the realm of pseudoscience and that they advance ineffective interventions, as well as their assertion that the increasing affinity toward EMTs among psychotherapists is a sort of occupational disorder that the field should take determined steps to counter. Moreover, we will establish that substantial evidence shows strong efficacy for EMTs, that theories underlying EMTs have an empirical basis, and that an affinity toward EMTs is compatible with critical thinking abilities.

Efficacy Research on EMTs for Psychological Issues

In framing their argument, Gaudiano et al. were explicit about their belief that EMTs are not research-supported:

> ...the only published, placebo-controlled studies of both EFT and TFT to date suggest that any benefits observed from the procedures are likely the result of placebo effects (p. 648).

Extensive research countering this assertion is readily available. The Association for Comprehensive Energy Psychology, for instance, posts regularly updated accounts of current research on EMT on its website (www.energypsych.org). Even a cursory review of this material would have provided the authors with the correct information that 18 randomized controlled trials (RCTs) investigating the two most widely used EMT methods (EFT and TFT) had been published by the time their article appeared. Twelve studies controlled for placebo effects by using either a placebo treatment or an active-ingredient comparison condition (the other controlled studies used wait-list comparison groups). All of these studies were published in peer-reviewed journals (see Table 1).

In each of the RCTs, tapping on a prescribed set of acupoints resulted in statistically significant improvement of the target condition. In 10 of 12 studies that used a placebo or active-ingredient comparison group, the treatment outperformed the comparison condition or was equivalent to an empirically established treatment (Baker & Siegel, 2010; Benor, Ledger, Toussaint, Hett, & Zaccaro,

2009; Church, 2009a; Church, Yount, & Brooks, 2012; Karatzias et al., 2011; Llewellyn-Edwards & Llewellyn-Edwards, 2012; Rubino, in press; Salas, Brooks, & Rowe, 2011; Sezgin & Özcan, 2009; Wells, Polglase, Andrews, Carrington, & Baker, 2003). In an 11th study (Pignotti, 2005), tapping on acupoints in a prescribed order produced equivalent improvement to tapping on acupoints in a random order. In only one of the 12 studies (Waite & Holder, 2003) did a pure placebo condition perform as well as tapping on prescribed acupoints, and a possible explanation was that even in the placebo condition, the subjects' acupoints were inadvertently being stimulated (Feinstein, 2009).

In 2012, Feinstein published an analysis of the 18 RCTs on dimensions such as the study's use of blinding, effect size, objective measures (vs. self-inventories only), active-ingredient (vs. wait-list only) comparison groups, and follow-up in each trial. Statistical significance was reported on at least one salient outcome measure in each of the RCTs. Sustained improvement was found in each of the eight studies that conducted follow-up investigation. The overall conclusion based on this analysis was that the RCTs "consistently demonstrated strong effect sizes and other positive statistical results that far exceed chance after relatively few treatment sessions" (Feinstein, 2012a, p. 14). In addition to the 18 RCTs, the review identified a total of 51 peer-reviewed papers that tracked outcomes following the use of TFT or EFT. All 51 papers reported positive changes in symptoms or behavior following the treatment, with moderate to large effect sizes being found where calculated. Three studies of patients with PTSD described a rapid reduction of symptoms from above to below PTSD thresholds on standardized self-inventories after a single session of the EMT being studied (Church, Piña, Reategui, & Brooks, 2011; Connolly & Sakai, 2011; Sakai, Connolly, & Oas, 2010).

A Sampling of Pertinent Studies

To illustrate the quality of the existing evidence, brief descriptions of some of the most pertinent studies follow. A comparison between EFT and Eye Movement Desensitization and Reprocessing (EMDR) in the treatment of PTSD was conducted by Scotland's National Health Service (Karatzias et al., 2011). Forty-six individuals who met *DSM-IV* criteria for PTSD were randomly assigned to EFT or EMDR treatment. EMDR is an established evidence-based treatment for PTSD (Bisson & Andrew, 2007), and this study was the first controlled comparison between EFT and EMDR for PTSD. Assessments included standardized self-report measures of PTSD symptoms, anxiety, depression, and satisfaction with life, and a clinician-administered PTSD scale. A baseline assessment was made 8 weeks prior to treatment, pretreatment, posttreatment, and 3 months after the completion of treatment. Assessors were blind to the treatment arm. Treatment fidelity was determined by videotapes of a sample of the sessions and was equivalent for both treatment conditions. Pre/posttreatment differences exceeded the .001 level of statistical significance on all measures for both treatment conditions, with strong effect sizes of d = .9 or higher on all measures. Participants were allowed up to eight 1-hour sessions. The EFT treatments were completed after an average of 3.8 sessions and the EMDR treatments after an average of 3.7 sessions. Overall, the study revealed that both interventions produced significant therapeutic gains at posttreatment and at 3-month follow-up. Weaknesses of the study included relatively small numbers (23 for each group), a high loss to follow-up, and lack of a no-treatment control.

In another study of PTSD, TFT was shown to rapidly relieve PTSD that had persisted more than a dozen years after the 1994 genocide in Rwanda. Sakai et al. (2010) treated 50 adolescents who were orphaned by the genocide and were still suffering from severe PTSD symptoms, including frequent flashbacks, nightmares, inability to concentrate, withdrawal, regression, and bedwetting. A standardized pre/posttreatment PTSD symptom inventory for parents or caregivers, translated into the local language in a manner approved by the test-makers, was completed by the orphanage staff for 181 adolescents. The 50 with the highest PTSD scores were selected for the study. The ratings for all 50 were above the PTSD cutoff. After a single TFT session, the caregivers' ratings on the same inventory showed 47 (94%) of them as being below the PTSD cutoff. On 1-year follow-up using the same instrument, 46 (92%) of the participants were still rated as being below the PTSD cutoff.

Connolly and Sakai (2011) then investigated the effects on PTSD symptoms of a single-session TFT treatment on 71 adult survivors of the 1994 Rwandan genocide compared to 74 adult survivors in a wait-list group. The study used a randomized

Table 1: *RCTs Using Standardized Measures to Investigate the Efficacy of TFT and EFT*[1]

Author (date)	Condition treated	Treatment/ Controls	*n*	Measures	Main findings/Comments
Baker & Siegel (2010)	Specific phobia (small animals)	**EFT** SC No Tx	11 10 10	BAT, BSSPP, FOSAQ, Pulse rate, SUD	A 45-minute EFT session produced significant decreases in fear on most measures. The control conditions did not. Benefits persisted on follow-up more than a year after the treatment.
Brattberg (2008)	Fibromyalgia	**EFT** Wait list	26 36	CPAQ, GSE, HAD, PCS, SF-36, SUD	An 8-week treatment program was administered over the Internet with e-mail support. Improvement on pain, anxiety, depression, and other measures was highly significant for the treatment group.
Church (2009a)	Basketball performance	**EFT** Inspirational talk by coach	13 13	Free throws, vertical jump height	Four 90-minute group EFT sessions with moderately to severely depressed college students in the Philippines reduced average depression scores from well above the moderate range to well below the depression cut-off.
Church, De Asis, & Brooks (2012)	Depression	**EFT** Wait List	9 9	Beck Depression Inventory	Male and female college basketball players significantly improved free-throw percentages after 15 minutes of EFT, compared to controls, but group differences on jump height were not significant.
Church, Hawk, et al. (2013)	PTSD	**EFT** Wait list	8 8	PCL-M, SA-45	Abused teenage boys in a facility in Peru scoring an average of 36 on the IES (35 indicates a "probable diagnosis of PTSD") scored an average of 3 after a single EFT session. Scores for the wait list group were unchanged.
Church, Piña, et al. (2011)	PTSD	**EFT** Wait List	29 25	Impact of Events Scale	PCL scores dropped from 61.4 to 34.6 after 6 EFT sessions (50 is the PTSD cutoff; 17 is the lowest score possible) and held at 36.5 on 6-month follow-up.
Church, Yount, et al. (2012)	Stress	**EFT** SC No Tx	28 28 27	SA-45, Salivary Cortisol Assay	Psychological symptoms decreased for both treatment conditions after a 1-hour session but significantly more for the EFT group. Significant drops in stress cortisol levels were found after EFT but not for the other two groups.
Connolly & Sakai (2011)	PTSD	**TFT** Wait list	71 74	Modified PTSD Symptom Scale, Trauma Symptom Inventory	Survivors of the 1994 genocide in Rwanda received a single TFT session (average 41 minutes) conducted by laypersons trained in TFT. Highly significant Improvement on all subscales held on 2-year follow-up.
Irgens et al. (2012)	Anxiety	**TFT** Wait list	24 24	Fear Survey, MINI, HAD, LSAS, SCL-90-R	Significant symptom reduction was found on most scales following one to eight sessions (mean = 3.6) in comparison to the control group.

Study	Condition	Treatment	n	Measures	Outcome
Jones et al. (2011)	Public speaking anxiety	**EFT** Wait list	18 18	PRCS, PRCA-24B, SRQ, STAI, SUD, TBC	Significant improvement was found on most of the scales after a 45-minute EFT session.
Karatzias et al. (2011)	PTSD	**EFT** EMDR	23 23	Clinician Administered PTSD Scale, HAD, PCL-C, SLS	Both treatment conditions showed highly significant improvements on self-report measures as well as interview assessments after a mean of 3.8 (EFT) or 3.7 (EMDR) sessions.
Llewellyn-Edwards & Llewellyn-Edwards (2012)	Soccer performance	**EFT** Instructions from trainer	7 8	Kicks at goal from 13.5 meters	Significant improvement was found on goal kicks after a group EFT session focusing on obstacles to kick accuracy but not after a coaching session aimed at improving accuracy.
Rubino (in press)	Test-taking anxiety	**EFT** DB/exposure Wait list	30 30 30	RTI, SA-45, Westside Test Anxiety Scale	Both treatments significantly reduced test-taking anxiety after 4 weeks of practice following a 2-hour training session in the method. High dropout rate, with 41 subjects completing the study.
Salas et al. (2011)	Specific phobias	**EFT** DB	11 11	BAT, Beck Anxiety Inventory, SUD	College students self-reporting specific phobias (heights, snakes, cockroaches, darkness, syringes) improved after a single brief session of either treatment, with EFT being statistically superior.
Schoninger & Hartung (2010)	Public speaking anxiety	**TFT** Wait list	28 20	Speaker Anxiety Scale, SUD	Highly significant reduction of anxiety and increase in measures of positive anticipation were found after a 1-hour session.
Sezgin & Özcan (2009)	Test-taking anxiety	**EFT** Progressive relaxation	35 35	Test Anxiety Inventory	Both treatments significantly reduced test-taking anxiety after 2 months of practice following an initial training session. EFT led to significantly greater improvement than the relaxation group.
Stapleton et al. (2012)	Food Cravings	**EFT** Wait list	49 47	BMI, Food Craving Inventory, PFS, SA-45	Reductions in food craving followed four 2-hour group sessions. Outcomes held at 1 year along with reduced body mass.
Wells et al. (2003)	Specific phobia (small animals)	**EFT** DB/Exposure	18 17	BAT, Pulse Rate, SFS, SUD	Both groups showed significant reductions in fear after a 30-minute session, with EFT being statistically superior to DB. Gains held on most measures 6 to 9 months after the treatment.

Note: [1]Adapted from Feinstein, 2012a.

Abbreviations: BAT = Behavior Approach Task; BSSPP = Brief Standard Self-Rating for Phobic Patients; BMI = Body Mass Index; CBT = Cognitive Behavior Therapy; CPAQ = Chronic Pain Acceptance Questionnaire; DB = Diaphragmatic Breathing; FOSAQ = Fear of Specific Animal Questionnaire; EFT = Emotional Freedom Techniques; EMDR = Eye Movement Desensitization and Reprocessing; GSE = General Self-Efficacy Scale; HAD = Hospital Anxiety and Depression Scale; LSAS = Liebowitz Social Anxiety Scale; MINI = Mini-International Neuropsychiatric Interview; NS = not specified; PCL-C = PTSD Checklist Civilian Version; PCS = Pain Catastrophizing Scale; PFS = Power of Food Scale; PRCA-24B = Personal Report of Communication Apprehension; PRCS = Personal Report of Confidence; RTI = Reactions to Tests Inventory; SA-45 = Symptom Assessment–45 Questionnaire; SC = Supportive Counseling; SCL-90-R = Symptom Checklist 90–Revised; SF-36 = Swedish Health Questionnaire; SFS = Standardized Fear Survey; SLS = Satisfaction with Life Scale; SRQ = Self-Report Questionnaire; STAI = State-Trait Anxiety Checklist; SUD = Subjective Units of Distress; TBC = Timed Behavior Checklist; TFT = Thought Field Therapy; TIR = Traumatic Incident Reduction; V/KD = Visual/Kinesthetic Dissociation; WHEE = Wholistic Hybrid Derived from EMDR and EFT.

wait-list comparison design with standardized self-inventories that assess PTSD symptoms and symptoms following trauma. Both inventories showed highly significant improvements that were sustained on 2-year follow-up. The investigators suggested additional research be conducted that utilizes a placebo or active-ingredient comparison group, noted that the findings from their sample do not necessarily generalize to all Rwandan genocide survivors, and acknowledged the possibility of missteps that may occur in cross-cultural research.

Church, Yount, and Brooks (2012) examined the changes in cortisol levels and psychological distress symptoms of 83 subjects randomly assigned to receive an EFT session, a supportive counseling session, or no treatment. Salivary cortisol assays were performed immediately before and 30 minutes after the intervention. Psychological distress was assessed using the Symptom Assessment–45 (SA-45), a 45-item standardized self-report inventory. The EFT group showed highly significant improvements on the SA-45 individual scales as well as on the two general scales: breadth of symptoms ($p < 0.001$) and depth of symptoms ($p < 0.001$). The EFT treated group experienced a 51% decrease in depth of symptoms whereas the counseling and control groups had a 17% and 14% decrease, respectively. When cortisol levels were compared, the EFT group showed a 24% decrease compared with 14% each in the other two groups. The authors concluded that "the decrease in cortisol levels in the EFT group mirrored the observed improvement in psychological distress" (p. 891).

In addition to the stress hormone levels examined by Church et al., other biological markers have also been tracked. Studies using quantitative electroencephalogram, electromyography, and other electrical devices showed that acupoint stimulation combined with the mental activation of scenes that evoke fear produces a rapid regulation of measures associated with the physiological fear response. These shifts also corresponded with self-reported reductions in fear following the treatment (Diepold & Goldstein, 2009; Lambrou, Pratt, & Chevalier, 2003; Swingle, Pulos, & Swingle, 2004; Swingle, 2010).

Selection of Studies by Gaudiano et al.

Ignoring most of these findings, Gaudiano et al. cited only the trials by Pignotti (2005) and Waite & Holder (2003). In these studies, tapping done in a different manner than prescribed by TFT (Pignotti) or EFT (Waite & Holder) performed as well as tapping that precisely followed the protocols. Gaudiano et al. interpreted these findings as showing that the positive outcomes seen in EMT therapies must be based on placebo effects. They do not address the fact that a remarkable 97% of participants in Pignotti's study, whether tapping on acupoints in a prescribed order or in a random order, "reported a complete elimination of all subjective emotional distress" (p. 38). Also omitted from their account was the finding that the act of tapping (in three variations) in Waite and Holder's study resulted in highly significant reductions in self-reported fear ($p < .003$, .001, and .001, respectively) while there was no improvement ($p = .255$) for those in a fourth arm that did not use any tapping. Waite and Holder (2003) attributed their unexpected findings to "characteristics [EFT] shares with more traditional therapies" (p. 25) such as desensitization and imaginal exposure, a conclusion that has been vigorously disputed (Baker & Carrington, 2005; Pasahow, 2010). Pignotti (2005) speculated on the possible roles of expectancy, social-demand characteristics, allegiance effects, and other placebo agents, as well as desensitization and imaginal exposure, in the outcomes of the two protocols she compared. While she concluded that the acupoint tapping was not an active ingredient in the treatment since these other, better-established explanations were available, she did not present any evidence showing that placebo, desensitization, and/or exposure have *ever* produced the "elimination of all subjective emotional distress" in 97% of the participants of a study.

Rather than citing the growing efficacy literature investigating EMTs, Gaudiano et al. rely on "a recent review of the literature [which] concluded that EMTs lack a valid scientific basis, show nonspecific efficacy, are not superior to other treatments, and display multiple characteristics of pseudoscience (Devilly, 2005)" (p. 649). This review, however, was published in 2005, prior to the preponderance of trials cited above. Furthermore, Devilly's review has been heavily criticized as "journalistic rather than embodying genuine scientific enquiry," engaging in "wildly speculative and sweeping generalizations" (Mollon, 2007a, p. 15). Mollon notes that the review utilizes "extensive disparagement of the motives and integrity of those who develop the newer therapies ... disregarding the more obvious and simpler hypothesis that the methods become popular because people find that they work" (p. 15). The review is neither "recent" in relationship to the relevant literature nor unbiased in relation to the studies it does review.

Attempt to Discredit Previous Efficacy Reviews

Gaudiano et al. do mention a review of the efficacy of EMTs that was published in *Psychotherapy: Theory, Research, Practice, Training*, a flagship clinical journal of the American Psychological Association (Feinstein, 2008), but their discussion is limited to a recounting of Pignotti and Thyer's (2009) critique of that paper, claiming bias and criticizing the fact that much of the research presented was from unpublished reports, dissertations, and conference proceedings. However, the 2008 review appeared in a special theme issue on *new* treatments. It did not attempt or claim to present only peer-reviewed RCTs. Instead, it organized the existing evidence into four useful categories: a) case studies, descriptions of systematic observation, or anecdotal reports (more than two thousand such reports were identified as being posted on websites or available from other sources); b) six outcome studies using standardized pre/post measures but no control group; c) four RCTs with "limited generalizability" (due to design flaws); and d) seven RCTs with "potentially strong generalizability." The paper clearly indicated which had appeared in peer-reviewed journals, which were dissertations, which were conference proceedings, and which (in the case of the anecdotal reports) were from websites. None of the studies were from "proprietary publications" or "promotional newsletters" as Gaudiano et al. imply.

Pignotti and Thyer (2009) pointed to the omission of three studies in Feinstein's 2008 review as "evidence of bias" (Gaudiano et al., 2012, p. 648). In a rejoinder, Feinstein (2009) explained that these studies had more bearing on mechanisms than efficacy issues, the focus of his review. He also noted that all three could be interpreted as showing positive outcomes following energy psychology protocols, lending further support for rather than countering the premises of his alleged biases. Pignotti and Thyer also claimed that Feinstein had been deceptive in not disclosing a conflict of interest—since he benefits from the fees for his books and trainings about the approach he was reviewing, another charge echoed by Gaudiano et al. Feinstein (2009) had responded that citing his "books and articles in the references, along with listing subtitles that clearly advocate an energy approach ... signaled to the reader [his] predispositions as the author, as did the tone of the writing" (p. 265). Beyond that, Feinstein stated, "I also did note on the journal's disclosure form 'a significant financial interest' in that 'I provide clinical services using this approach, have written three books on the topic, and consult and speak on the topic'" (p. 265). These clarifications appeared in the same issue as the Pignotti and Thyer critique cited by Gaudiano et al. but were not acknowledged in their comments. Uncritical citation of personal attacks on proponents of EMTs (e.g., Devilly, 2005; Pignotti & Thyer, 2009) obscures the most pertinent observation about the literature on the efficacy of EMTs, which is that the research since Feinstein's review of the preliminary evidence has supported his initial assessments (Feinstein, 2012a; Gruder, 2012).

Empirical Support for Theories Underlying EMTs

Beyond claiming that there is no efficacy research supporting EMTs, Gaudiano et al. assert that "no scientific evidence to date has been offered to support the theory underlying any EMTs" (p. 648). This is also not the case (e.g., Feinstein 2010, 2012b; Lane, 2009; Ruden, 2005, 2010). For instance, evidence cited by Feinstein (2012b) suggests that the stimulation of acupuncture points during imaginal exposure activates (a) electromagnetic signals that reduce threat arousal in the amygdala (Dhond, Kettner, & Napadow, 2007; Fang et al., 2009; Hui et al., 2005), (b) delta waves that are believed to depotentiate neural pathways that maintain maladaptive fear (Harper, 2012), and (c) electromagnetic fields that organize neural activity (Buschman, Denovellis, Diogo, Bullock, & Miller, 2012).

Electromagnetic fields have been shown to direct cellular activity in wound healing (e.g., Liboff, 2004; Oschman, 2000), and recent studies have demonstrated that oscillations in the electromagnetic fields of the prefrontal cortex impact thought and behavior (Buschman et al., 2012).

Referring back to Karl Lashley's (1950) speculation that memory recall must involve "some sort of resonance among a very large number of neurons" (p. 479), Feinstein notes that recent neurological findings are showing how large-scale electrical oscillations across distant brain regions allow "content-specific information to be transmitted" (Feinstein, 2012b, p. 71). These findings help explain the longstanding enigma of how diverse brain activities involved in information processing are coordinated. Energy psychology interventions are believed to impact the electromagnetic fields that coordinate activity among neurons.

In addition to disregarding studies focusing specifically on the mechanisms of energy psychology, Gaudiano et al. dismiss without mention the extensive, if still somewhat controversial (e.g., Ernst, 2006; Stux & Hammerschlag, 2001) literature investigating the nature of the acupuncture points and meridians that are at the core of EMT theory. While it is impossible to begin to do justice to the thousands of research studies published on acupuncture and other energy therapies (e.g., Benor, 2004; Deadman & Al-Khafaj, 2007; Gerber, 2001; Oschman, 2000; Swanson, 2010; World Health Organization, 2003), a few salient examples are mentioned here.

Attempts to scientifically establish the anatomy of the meridian system, first described in papers by Kim Bonghan in North Korea in the 1960s, have been corroborated by independent investigators in other countries (Johng et al., 2007; Langevin & Yandow, 2002; Milbradt, 2009; Schlebusch, Maric-Oehler, & Popp, 2005; Yan et al., 1992). Heat, sensations, and radiolabeled traces propagate along the meridian lines described in traditional Chinese texts (Darras, de Vernejoul, & Albarede, 1992; Ji, 1981). Low electrical impedance, a characteristic of many acupuncture points (Ahn, 2008; Johng et al., 2002), is believed to make these points more responsive in producing the electrochemical effects of acupuncture. Acupuncture has, for instance, been shown to stimulate the release of endogenous opioids in brainstem, subcortical, and limbic structures (Han, 2003; Pomeranz, 1996), increase the brain's opioid binding potential (Harris, Zubieta, Scott, Napadow, Gracely, & Clauw, 2009), deactivate limbic arousal (Fang et al., 2009), stimulate the release of adenosine (Goldman et al., 2010), and create an anti-inflammatory response via secretion of adrenocorticotropic hormone from the pituitary gland (Li et al., 2008). This brief sampling from a much larger literature shows that, unlike Gaudiano et al.'s assertion to the contrary, considerable evidence supporting the theories underlying EFTs is available.

Characteristics of Psychotherapists Utilizing EMTs

From ignoring the preponderance of evidence and portraying EMTs as unsubstantiated by empirical studies or plausible theory, Gaudiano et al. proceed to investigate the characteristics of psychotherapists who would utilize such supposedly questionable methods. As would be expected, given that EMTs are alternative therapies, psychotherapists who employ EMTs showed more positive attitudes toward alternative therapies. The other characteristics listed, however, become confounded with ideological issues, such as whether relying on intuition is a positive or negative trait in a clinician. The authors' approach to assessing "erroneous health beliefs" is deeply bound in ideological assumptions. The assumption that endorsing "erroneous health beliefs that are not supported by scientific evidence" (p. 650) is a negative characteristic hinges, for instance, on another assumption, which is that the health beliefs are actually erroneous. The first item on the 10-item Health Beliefs Subscale (Lindeman, Keskivaara, & Roschier, 2000) used by the authors to determine "erroneous health beliefs" is:

> *An imbalance between energy currents lies behind many illnesses.*

This "erroneous" health belief has been a basic tenet of acupuncture, the original EMT, for several thousand years. It was first affirmed within a Western scientific framework in the 1940s (Langman & Burr, 1947). Langman and Burr found that voltage abnormalities around the cervix predicted malignancies with 85% accuracy in more than 1000 women presenting with gynecological problems. Many cardiac conditions, including cardiac arrhythmias (Spragg & Tomaselli, 2011), are due to abnormal electrical activity in the heart. Neurological conditions, such as seizure disorders (Lowenstein, 2011), involve imbalances in underlying electrical currents. Anxiety disorders (Drevets, Charney, & Rauch, 2009) and mood disorders (Savitz & Drevets, 2009) reflect imbalances in affective circuitry and stability. Scoring, as an erroneous health belief, agreement with the statement "an imbalance between energy currents lies behind many illnesses" is an ideological position rather than an example of the critical thinking the authors extol.

The ideological bias evidenced in their assessment of "erroneous health beliefs," as well as in the selection of literature that supports their own beliefs regarding EMTs while neglecting to acknowledge the strong body of evidence that contradicts their beliefs, led the authors of the current paper to question and scrutinize the validity of the items in the Critical Thinking Questionnaire used by Gaudiano et al. (selected by Sharp, Herbert, & Redding, 2008, from other critical thinking assessment instruments). The first of the eight items is:

> Imagine that disorder X occurs in one in every 1,000 people. Imagine also there is a test to diagnose the disorder that always gives a positive result when a person has the disorder. Finally, imagine that the test has a false positive rate of 5 percent. This means that the test wrongly indicates that the disorder is present in 5 percent of the cases where the person does not have the disorder. Imagine that we choose a person randomly, administer the test, and that it yields a positive result (indicates that the person has the disorder). What is the probability that the individual actually has the disorder, assuming that we know nothing else about the individual's psychological or medical history?
>
> Choices: A) <10% B) 10–30% C) 30–50% D) 50–70% E) 70–90% F) >90%

While certainly calling for skills in critical thinking, such skills will not be detected if the clinician taking the test does not possess the requisite statistical training and mathematical ability to calculate probabilities. Critical thinking tests are, in fact, notoriously problematic (Ennis, 1993). Ennis, who designed one of the instruments from which items were selected in the Gaudiano et al. study, notes that most tests are simply not comprehensive enough to adequately assess critical thinking skills. Moreover, "differences in background beliefs and assumptions between test maker and test taker [can] result in justifiably different answers to test questions" (Ennis, 1993, p. 181). Gaudiano et al., on the other hand, do their Internet-based survey using eight items adapted from a 28-item inventory whose questions were themselves selected from "several established measures of critical thinking" (Sharp, 2003, p. 36). Validity or reliability evaluations of either the eight-item or 28-item inventories are not cited. Gaudiano et al. conclude that the EMT therapists "demonstrated lower critical thinking abilities" (p. 650) than other therapists without acknowledging the complexities involving measures of critical thinking, the potential impact of differing background beliefs between test maker and test taker, or possible distortions resulting from an unvalidated assessment tool.

Conclusion

The great irony in the article by Gaudiano et al. is that critical thinking would compel informed therapists to seriously consider incorporating EMTs into their practices, based on the 51 peer-reviewed papers mentioned above that show positive, lasting, and, often, unusually rapid outcomes. Even though the evidence suggests that EMTs hold strong promise for better patient care, "Tapping Their Patients' Problems Away" attempts—using obsolete data and sardonic characterizations of EMT therapists—to steer clinicians and researchers away from EMTs. Its lead author has, in fact, for more than a decade, been sounding the alarm that EMTs "are gaining widespread acceptance among mental health practitioners, despite their frankly bizarre theories and techniques, extraordinary claims, and absence of scientific support" (Gaudiano & Herbert, 2000, p. 29). This brings us to a second irony. Most of us writing this rebuttal would, in 2000, have agreed with him.

In 2000, a small group of proponents of EMTs—who felt certain about the unproven clinical benefits of EMTs for rapidly and deeply releasing anxieties, fears, phobias, PTSD, cravings, and more—were zealous in their claims and expressing annoyance at requests for empirical evidence. This seeming arrogance—combined with the strange-looking procedures, stranger explanatory models, and public assertions with no research support—did not endear the approach to the clinical community. A dozen years later, however, 42% of the psychotherapists in Gaudiano et al.'s sample indicated frequent or probable use of EMTs, and the research evidence is tending to affirm rather than contradict the "extraordinary claims" and "bizarre" techniques of the early EMT proponents. Of the 51 papers presenting positive outcomes of EMT interventions referred to above, 50 have been published since 2000; 39 in the past four years. This profusion of new data invites the other 58% of the clinical community, including Gaudiano et al., to reexamine EMTs.

Achieving a balance between sound skepticism and receptivity to untested health care innovations is notoriously challenging (Forman, 1981). For instance, the cure for scurvy was known to the British admiralty for more than a century before it was adopted. Another tragic historical example of established beliefs overpowering receptivity to medical innovation is in the way that physicians did not begin to sanitize their hands and equipment prior to surgery until decades after it had been demonstrated that these practices save lives. The existing research on energy psychology suggests that an innovation has been developed that promises to bring about unusually rapid improvement for a range of conditions. Its compatibility with established scientific principles and clinical procedures, as discussed in this paper (also see Church, 2009b), adds plausibility to this prospect. Given the widespread suffering psychotherapists are called upon to help alleviate, and the ever-pressing need for more powerful nonpharmaceutical treatments, it behooves the psychotherapy community to continue to advance the best evidence-based therapies while also encouraging innovations by sincere clinicians who seek solutions outside mainstream paradigms.

References

Ahn, A. C., Colbert, A. P., Anderson, B. J., Martinsen, Ø. G., Hammerschlag, R., Cina, S., & Langevin, H.M. (2008). Electrical properties of acupuncture points and meridians: A systematic review. *Bioelectromagnetics, 29*, 245–256.

Baker, A. H., & Carrington, P. (2005). A comment on Waite and Holder's research supposedly invalidating EFT. Retrieved November 25, 2012, from http://energypsych.org/displaycommon.cfm?an=1&subarticlenbr=7

Baker, A. H., & Siegel, M. A. (2010). Emotional Freedom Techniques (EFT) reduces intense fears: A partial replication and extension of Wells et al. *Energy Psychology: Theory, Research, and Treatment, 2*(2), 13–30.

Benor, D. J. (2004). *Consciousness, bioenergy, and healing* (Vol. II, *Healing research*, professional edition). Bellmawr, NJ: Wholistic Healing Publications.

Benor, D. J., Ledger, K., Toussaint, L., Hett, G., & Zaccaro, D. (2009). Pilot study of Emotional Freedom Techniques, Wholistic Hybrid Derived from Eye Movement Desensitization and Reprocessing and Emotional Freedom Techniques, and cognitive behavioral therapy for treatment of test anxiety in university students. *Explore: The Journal of Science and Healing, 5*, 338–340. doi:10.1016/j.explore.2009.08.001

Bisson, J., & Andrew, M. (2007). Psychological treatment of post-traumatic stress disorder (PTSD). *Cochrane Database of Systematic Reviews*, Issue 3. Art. No.: CD003388. doi:10.1002/14651858.CD003388.pub3.

Brattberg, G. (2008). Self-administered EFT (Emotional Freedom Techniques) in individuals with fibromyalgia: A randomized trial: *Integrative Medicine: A Clinician's Journal, 7*(4), 30–35.

Buschman, T. J., Denovellis, E. L., Diogo, C., Bullock, D., & Miller, E. K. (2012). Synchronous oscillatory neural ensembles for rules in the prefrontal cortex. *Neuron, 76*, 838–846. doi:10.1016/j.neuron.2012.09.029

Callahan, R. J., & Callahan, J. (1996). *Thought Field Therapy (TFT) and trauma: Treatment and theory.* Indian Wells, CA: Thought Field Therapy Training Center.

Church, D. (2009a). The effect of EFT (Emotional Freedom Techniques) on athletic performance: A randomized controlled blind trial. *Open Sports Sciences Journal, 2*, 94–99. doi:10.2174/1875399X00902010094

Church, D. (2009b). Fighting the fire: Emotions, evolution, and the future of psychology [Editorial]. *Energy Psychology: Theory, Research, and Treatment, 1*(1), 9–14.

Church, D., & Brooks, A. (2010). Application of Emotional Freedom Techniques. *Integrative Medicine: A Clinician's Journal, 9*(4), 46–48.

Church, D., De Asis, M. A., & Brooks, A. J. (2012). Brief group intervention using Emotional Freedom Techniques for depression in college students: A randomized controlled trial. *Depression Research and Treatment* [Online journal]. doi:10.1155/2012/257172

Church, D., Hawk, C., Brooks, A., Toukolehto, O., Wren, M., Dinter, I., & Stein, P. (2013). Psychological trauma in veterans using Emotional Freedom Techniques: A randomized controlled trial. *Journal of Nervous and Mental Disease, 201*, 153–160.

Church, D., Piña, O., Reategui, C., & Brooks, A. (2011). Single session reduction of the intensity of traumatic memories in abused adolescents after EFT: A randomized controlled pilot study. *Traumatology, 18*, 73–79. doi:10.1177/1534765611426788

Church, D., Yount, G., & Brooks, A. (2012). The effect of Emotional Freedom Techniques (EFT) on stress biochemistry: A randomized controlled trial. *Journal of Nervous and Mental Disease, 200*, 891–896. doi:10.1097/NMD.0b013e31826b9fc1

Connolly, S., & Sakai, C. (2011). Brief trauma intervention with Rwandan genocide survivors using Thought Field Therapy. *International Journal of Emergency Mental Health, 13*(3), 161–172.

Darras, J. C., de Vernejoul, P., & Albarede, P. (1992). Nuclear medicine and acupuncture: A study on the migration of radioactive tracers after injection at acupoints. *American Journal of Acupuncture, 20*, 245–256.

Deadman, P., & Al-Khafaj, M. (2007). A manual of acupuncture (2nd ed.). East Sussex, England: Journal of Chinese Medicine Publications.

Devilly, G. J. (2005). Power therapies and possible threats to the science of psychology and psychiatry. *Australian and New Zealand Journal of Psychiatry, 39*, 437–445.

Dhond, R. P., Kettner, N., & Napadow, V. (2007). Neuroimaging acupuncture effects in the human brain. *Journal of Alternative and Complementary Medicine. 13*, 603–616.

Diepold, J. H., & Goldstein, D. (2009). Thought field therapy and QEEG changes in the treatment of trauma: A case study. *Traumatology, 15*, 85–93. doi:10.1177/1534765608325304

Drevets, W. C., Charney, D. S., & Rauch, S. L. (2009). Neuroimaging and the neuroanatomical circuits implicated in anxiety, fear, and stress-induced circuitry disorders. In B. J. Sadock, V. A. Sadock, & P. Ruiz (Eds.), *Kaplan and Sadock's comprehensive textbook of psychiatry* (9th ed., pp. 1881–1898). Philadelphia, PA: Lippincott, Williams, & Wilkins.

Ennis, R. H. (1993). Critical thinking assessment. *Theory into Practice, 32*, 179–186.

Ernst, E. (2006). Acupuncture—a critical analysis. *Journal of Internal Medicine, 259*, 125–137.

Fang, J., Jin, Z., Wang, Y., Li, K., Kong, J., Nixon, E. E., & Hui, K. K-S. (2009). The salient characteristics of the central effects of acupuncture needling: Limbic-paralimbic-neocortical network modulation. *Human Brain Mapping, 30*, 1196–1206.

Feinstein, D. (2008). Energy psychology: A review of the preliminary evidence. *Psychotherapy: Theory, Research, Practice, Training, 45*, 199–213.

Feinstein, D. (2009). Facts, paradigms, and anomalies in the acceptance of energy psychology: A rejoinder to McCaslin's (2009) and Pignotti and Thyer's (2009) comments on Feinstein (2008a). *Psychotherapy: Theory, Research, Practice, Training. 46*, 262–269. doi:10.1037/a0016086

Feinstein, D. (2010). Rapid treatment of PTSD: Why psychological exposure with acupoint tapping may be effective. *Psychotherapy: Theory, Research, Practice, Training. 47*(3), 385–402. doi:10.1037/a0021171

Feinstein, D. (2012a). Acupoint stimulation in treating psychological disorders: Evidence of efficacy. *Review of General Psychology.* Advance online publication. doi:10.1037/a0028602

Feinstein, D. (2012b). What does *energy* have to do with energy psychology? *Energy Psychology: Theory, Research, and Treatment, 4*(2), 59–80.

Forman, R. (1981). Medical resistance to innovation. *Medical Hypotheses, 7*, 1009–1017.

Gaudiano, B. A., Brown, L. A., & Miller, I. W. (2012). Tapping their patients' problems away?: Characteristics of psychotherapists using energy meridian techniques. *Research on Social Work Practice, 22*, 647–655. doi:10.1177/1049731512448468

Gaudiano, B. A., & Herbert, J. D. (2000). Can we really tap our problems away?: A critical analysis of Thought Field Therapy. *Skeptical Inquirer, 24*, 29–36.

Gerber, R. (2001). *Vibrational healing* (3rd ed.). Rochester, VT: Bear & Co.

Goldman, N., Chen, M., Fujita, T., Xu, Q., Peng, W., Liu, W., ... & Nedergaard, M. (2010). Adenosine A1 receptors mediate local anti-nociceptive effects of acupuncture. *Nature Neuroscience, 13*, 883–888.

Gruder, D. (2012). Controversial 2008 research review published in *Psychotherapy* finds new support. *Psychotherapy Bulletin, 47*(3), 39–42.

Han, J. S. (2003). Acupuncture: Neuropeptide release produced by electrical stimulation of different frequencies. *Trends in Neuroscience, 26*, 17–22.

Harper, M. (2012). Taming the amygdala: An EEG analysis of exposure therapy for the traumatized. *Traumatology, 18*(2), 61–74.

Harris, R. E., Zubieta, J. K., Scott, D. J., Napadow, V., Gracely, R. H., & Clauw, D. J. (2009). Traditional Chinese acupuncture and placebo (sham) acupuncture are differentiated by their effects on mu-opioid receptors (MORs). *Neuroimage, 47*, 1077–1085.

Hui, K. K.-S., Liu, J., Marina, O., Napadow, V., Haselgrove, C., Kwong, K. K., & Makris, N. (2005). The integrated response of the human cerebro-cerebellar and limbic systems to acupuncture stimulation at ST 36 as evidenced by fMRI. *NeuroImage, 27*, 479–496.

Irgens, A., Uldal M., & Hoffart, A. (2012). Thought Field Therapy (TFT) as a treatment for anxiety symptoms: A randomized controlled trial. *Explore: The Journal of Science and Healing, 8*(6), 331–338. doi:10.1016/j.explore.2012.08.002.

Ji, Z. P. (1981). Studies on propagated sensation along channels. *Journal of Traditional Chinese Medicine, 1*, 3–6.

Johng H.-M., Cho, J. H., Shin, H. S., Soh, K. S., Koo, T. H., Choi, S. Y., & Park, M. S. (2002). Frequency dependence of impedances at the acupuncture point Quze (PC3). *IEEE Engineering in Medicine and Biology, 21*, 33–36.

Johng, H.-M., Yoo, J. S., Yoon, T.-J., Shin, H.-S., Lee, B.-C., Lee, C., ... & Soh, K.-S. (2007). Use of magnetic nanoparticles to visualize threadlike structures inside lymphatic vessels of rats. *Evidence Based Complementary and Alternative Medicine, 4*, 77–82. doi:10.1093/ecam/nel057

Jones, S., Thornton, J., & Andrews, H. (2011). Efficacy of EFT in reducing public speaking anxiety: A randomized controlled trial. *Energy Psychology: Theory, Research, and Treatment, 3*(1), 19–32.

Karatzias, T., Power, K., Brown, K., McGoldrick, T., Begum, M., Young, J, ... & Adams, S. (2011). A controlled comparison of the effectiveness and efficiency of two psychological therapies for posttraumatic stress disorder: Eye Movement Desensitization and Reprocessing vs. Emotional Freedom Techniques. *Journal of Nervous and Mental Disease, 199*, 372–378. doi:10.1097/NMD.0b013e31821cd262

Lambrou, P. T., Pratt, G. J., & Chevalier, G. (2003). Physiological and psychological effects of a mind/body therapy on claustrophobia. *Subtle Energies and Energy Medicine, 14*, 239–251.

Lane, J. (2009). The Neurochemistry of counterconditioning: Acupressure desensitization in psychotherapy. *Energy Psychology: Theory, Research, and Treatment, 1*(1), 31–44.

Langevin, H.M., & Yandow, J.A. (2002). Relationship of acupuncture points and meridians to connective tissue planes. *Anatomical Record, 269*, 257–265.

Langman, L., & Burr, H. S. (1947). Electrometric studies in women with malignancy of cervix uteri. *Science, 105*(2721), 209–210.

Lashley, K. S. (1950). In search of the engram. In *Physiological mechanisms in animal behavior* (Society for Experimental Biology, Society's Symposium IV, pp. 454–482). Oxford, England: Academic Press.

Li, A., Lao, L., Wang, Y., Xin, J., Ren, K., Berman, B. M., ... & Zhang, R. (2008). Electroacupuncture activates corticotrophin-releasing hormone-containing neurons in the paraventricular nucleus of the hypothalamus to alleviate edema in a rat model of inflammation. *BioMed Central Complementary and Alternative Medicine, 8*, 20–25.

Liboff, A.R. (2004). Toward an electromagnetic paradigm for biology and medicine. *Journal of Alternative and Complementary Medicine. 10*(1), 41–47.

Lindeman, M., Keskivaara, P., & Roschier, M. (2000). Assessment of magical beliefs about food and health. *Journal of Health Psychology, 5*, 195–209.

Llewellyn-Edwards, T., & Llewellyn-Edwards, M. (2012, Spring). The effect of *EFT* (Emotional Freedom Techniques) on soccer performance. *Fidelity: Journal for the National Council of Psychotherapy, 47*, 14–19.

Lohr, J. M. (2001). Sakai et al. is not an adequate demonstration of TFT effectiveness. *Journal of Clinical Psychology, 57*, 1229–1235. doi:10.1002/jclp.1089

Lowenstein, D. H. (2011). Seizures and epilepsy. In D. L. Longo, A. S., Fauci, D. L., Kasper, S. L., Hauser, J. L. Jameson, & J. Loscalzo (Eds.), *Harrison's principles of internal medicine* (18th ed., pp. 3251–3270). New York, NY: McGraw-Hill Professional.

McNally, R. J. (2001). Tertullian's motto and Callahan's method. *Journal of Clinical Psychology, 57*, 1171–1174. doi:10.1002/jclp.1083

Milbradt, D. (2009). Bonghan channels in acupuncture. *Acupuncture Today, 10*(4). Retrieved from http://www.acupuncturetoday.com/mpacms/at/article.php?id=31918

Mollon, P. (2007a). Debunking the pseudoscience debunkers. *Clinical Psychology Forum* (a monthly publication of the British Psychological Society's Division of Clinical Psychology), Issue *174*, 13–16.

Mollon, P. (2007b). Thought Field Therapy and its derivatives: Rapid relief of mental health problems through tapping on the body. *Primary Care and Community Psychiatry, 12*, 123–127.

Murray, B. (1999). APA no longer approves CE sponsorship for Thought Field Therapy. *APA Monitor, 30*(11), 5.

Oschman, J. L. (2000). *Energy medicine: The scientific basis.* New York, NY: Harcourt.

Pasahow, R. (2010). Methodological problems in Waite and Holder (2003) preclude meaningful interpretations about Emotional Freedom Techniques (EFT). *Energy Psychology: Theory, Research, and Treatment, 2*(2), 57–72.

Pignotti, M. (2005). Thought Field Therapy Voice Technology vs. random meridian point sequences: A single-blind controlled experiment. *The Scientific Review of Mental Health Practice, 4*(1), 72–81.

Pignotti, M., & Thyer, B. (2009). Some comments on "Energy Psychology: A Review of the Evidence": Premature conclusions based on incomplete evidence? *Psychotherapy: Research, Practice, Training, 46*, 257–261.

Pomeranz, B. (1996). Scientific research into acupuncture for the relief of pain. *Journal of Alternative and Complementary Medicine, 2*, 53–60.

Ruden, R.A. (2005). A neurobiological basis for the observed peripheral sensory modulation of emotional responses. *Traumatology 11*(3), 145–158.

Ruden, R. A. (2010). *When the past is always present: Emotional traumatization, causes, and cures.* New York, NY: Routledge.

Rubino, A. (in press). The effectiveness of Emotional Freedom Techniques for optimal test performance. *Energy Psychology: Theory, Practice, and Research.*

Sakai, C. S., Connolly, S. M., & Oas, P. (2010). Treatment of PTSD in Rwandan genocide survivors using Thought Field Therapy. *International Journal of Emergency Mental Health, 12*(1), 41–50.

Salas, M., Brooks, A., & Rowe, J. (2011). The immediate effect of a brief energy psychology intervention (Emotional Freedom Techniques) on specific phobias: A pilot study. *Explore: The Journal of Science and Healing, 7*, 155–161.

Savitz, J. B., & Drevets, W. C. (2009). Brain circuits in major depressive disorder and bipolar disorder. In B. J. Sadock, V. A. Sadock, & P. Ruiz (Eds.), *Kaplan and Sadock's comprehensive textbook of psychiatry* (9th ed., pp. 1675–1686). Philadelphia, PA: Lippincott, Williams, & Wilkins.

Schlebusch, K.P., Maric-Oehler, W., & Popp, F. A. (2005). Biophotonics in the infrared spectral range reveal acupuncture meridian structure of the body. *Journal of Alternative and Complementary Medicine, 11*, 171–173.

Schoninger, B., & Hartung, J. (2010). Changes on self-report measures of public speaking anxiety following treatment with Thought Field Therapy. *Energy Psychology: Theory, Research, and Treatment, 2*(1), 13–26. doi:10.9769.EPJ.2010.2.1.BS

Sezgin, N., & Özcan, B. (2009). The effect of progressive muscular relaxation and Emotional Freedom Techniques on test anxiety in high school students: A randomized blind controlled study. *Energy Psychology: Theory, Research, and Treatment, 1*(1), 23–29.

Sharp, I. R. (2003). The role of critical thinking skills in practicing psychologists' theoretical orientation and choice of intervention techniques (Unpublished doctoral dissertation). Drexel University, Philadelphia, PA. Retrieved November 17, 2012, from http://idea.library.drexel.edu/bitstream/1860/250/7/sharp_thesis.pdf

Sharp, I. R., Herbert, J. D., & Redding, R. (2008). The role of critical thinking in practicing psychologists' theoretical orientation and choice of intervention techniques. *Scientific Review of Mental Health Practice, 6*, 21–30.

Spragg, D. D., & Tomaselli, G. F. (2011). Principles of electrophysiology. In D. L. Longo, A. S. Fauci, D. L. Kasper, S. L. Hauser, J. L. Jameson, & J. Loscalzo (Eds.), *Harrison's principles of internal medicine* (18th ed., pp. 1860–1866). New York, NY: McGraw-Hill Professional.

Stapleton, P., Sheldon, T., & Porter, B. (2012). Clinical benefits of Emotional Freedom Techniques on food cravings 12-months follow-up: A randomized controlled trial. *Energy Psychology: Theory, Research, and Treatment, 4*(1), 13–24.

Stux, G., & Hammerschlag, R. (2001). *Clinical acupuncture: Scientific basis.* New York, NY: Springer.

Swanson, C. (2010). *Life force: The scientific basis.* Tucson, AZ: Poseidia.

Swingle, P. (2010). Emotional Freedom Techniques (EFT) as an effective adjunctive treatment in the neurotherapeutic treatment of seizure disorders. *Energy Psychology: Theory, Research, and Treatment, 2*(1), 29–38.

Swingle, P. G., Pulos, L., & Swingle, M. K. (2004). Neurophysiological indicators of EFT treatment of posttraumatic stress. *Subtle Energies and Energy Medicine, 15*, 75–86.

Waite, L. W., & Holder, M. D. (2003). Assessment of the Emotional Freedom Technique: An alternative treatment for fear. *Scientific Review of Mental Health Practice, 2*(1) 20–26.

Wells, S., Polglase, K., Andrews, H. B., Carrington, P., & Baker, A. H. (2003). Evaluation of a meridian-based intervention, Emotional Freedom Techniques (EFT), for reducing specific phobias of small animals. *Journal of Clinical Psychology, 59*, 943–966. doi:10.1002/jclp.10189

World Health Organization. (2003). Acupuncture: Review and analysis of reports on controlled clinical trials. Geneva, Switzerland: Author.

Yan, Z., Chi, Y., Wang, P., Cheng, J., Wang, Y., Shu, Q., & Huang, G. (1992). Studies on the luminescence of channels in rats and its law of changes with "syndromes" and treatment of acupuncture and moxibustion. *Journal of Traditional Chinese Medicine, 12*, 283–287.

REVIEW ARTICLE

Old Wine in New Bottles: Response to Sise et al. (2014)

Brandon A. Gaudiano, Alpert Medical School of Brown University and Butler Hospital

Lily A. Brown, University of California, Los Angeles

Ivan W. Miller, Alpert Medical School of Brown University and Butler Hospital

We wish to thank the Editor for the opportunity to review the commentary by Sise and colleagues (2014) concerning our article on the characteristics of therapists who report using energy therapies, which was originally published in *Research on Social Work Practice* (Gaudiano, Brown, & Miller, 2012). Not surprisingly, Sise et al. disagree with our conclusions presented in this previous article about the continued lack of independently replicated, placebo-controlled research supporting the practice of energy therapy and the importance of the disconfirming evidence that exists to date. However, we do not believe that Sise et al. raise any additional points or new arguments that have not already been adequately addressed in our original article, and thus a detailed response is unnecessary at this time. Instead, we would refer readers back to a previously published critique by Pignotti and Thyer (2009), who provide a detailed rebuttal to many of the substantive points repeated by Sise et al in their current commentary.

References

Gaudiano, B. A., Brown, L. A., & Miller, I. W. (2012). Tapping their patients' problems away? Characteristics of psychotherapists using energy meridian techniques. *Research on Social Work Practice, 22*, 647–655.

Pignotti, M., & Thyer, B. (2009). Some comments on "Energy Psychology: A Review of the Evidence": Premature conclusions based on incomplete evidence? *Psychotherapy: Theory, Research, Practice, Training, 46*, 257–261.

Sise, M., Leskowitz, E., Stein, P. K., & Tranguch, A. (2014). Critical Thinking in the Energy Therapies: Comments on Gaudiano et al. (2012). *Energy Psychology: Theory, Research, and Treatment.*

ORIGINAL ABSTRACT

Reference: Bakker, G. M. (2013). The current status of energy psychology: Extraordinary claims with less than ordinary evidence. *Clinical Psychologist, 17*(3), 91–99. doi:10.1111/cp.12020

Proponents of energy psychology techniques, such as Thought Field Therapy and Emotional Freedom Techniques, have sought "empirically supported therapy" status despite an unsupported and implausible theoretical basis and claims in response of representing a "pseudoscientific" movement. Two major reviews of the supportive evidence which has accumulated over the past 30 years have been published recently. This current status report describes the history, theory, techniques, claims, and implications of the energy psychology movement, examines support for its theoretical base, its current outcome study support, and offers conclusions and recommendations as to its research and clinical prospects. It is concluded that there is scant support for the radical theories underlying energy psychology techniques, and that empirical support for their efficacy is methodologically weak, and has not been able to demonstrate an effect beyond nonspecific or placebo effects, or the incorporation of known-effective elements. The only dismantling studies to date have been disconfirmatory. Further research is highly unlikely to be scientifically productive, and scientist practitioners are advised to continue to adhere to well-established cognitive and behavioral principles.

Key Points

1. A review of empirical support for energy psychology treatments reveals it to be methodologically weak.
2. The theoretical basis of energy psychology is unsupported by research, such as dismantling studies of its techniques, and is highly implausible.
3. Energy psychology qualifies as a pseudoscience, and is not a research priority or a justified clinical option.

REVIEW ARTICLE

Comment on "The Current Status of Energy Psychology": Growing Evidence for Extraordinary Claims

David Feinstein

Abstract

In "The Current Status of Energy Psychology: Extraordinary Claims with Less than Ordinary Evidence," Bakker (2013) maintains that energy psychology rests on "an unsupported and implausible theoretical basis" (p. 1). He further asserts that attempts to establish empirical support for the efficacy of energy psychology have "not been able to demonstrate an effect beyond nonspecific or placebo effects, or the incorporation of known effective elements" (p. 1). This rejoinder will demonstrate that Bakker's selection and reporting skews his data toward these assertions and that a more balanced review would conclude that a) scientific support for the efficacy of energy psychology is accumulating; b) initial findings suggest, in fact, that the method is surprisingly rapid and effective; and c) plausible mechanisms for the documented positive outcomes are consistent with established psychological principles and have been described in the literature.

Keywords: amygdala, Emotional Freedom Techniques (EFT), energy psychology, memory reconsolidation, Thought Field Therapy (TFT)

Correspondence: David Feinstein, PhD, 777 East Main Street, Ashland, OR 97520. Tel: 541-482-1800; Fax: 772-382-8555; Email: df777@earthlink.net. **Disclosure:** By way of disclosure of potential conflicts of interest, the author conducts trainings, provides clinical services, and has written books and articles related to the approach examined in this paper.

Key Points

1. A recent "status report" on energy psychology claimed it to be unsupported by sound research and to lack a plausible theoretical basis.
2. A critical review of that report shows it to have omitted or discounted substantial evidence that contradicts its conclusions about both the efficacy of the approach and its theoretical foundation.
3. Preliminary evidence, in fact, suggests that energy psychology protocols are surprising in their speed and success rates with a range of psychological disorders and that the mechanisms involved can be explained by established psychological and scientific principles.

Energy psychology, in its most commonly practiced format, combines imaginal exposure and other cognitive procedures with the manual stimulation of acupuncture points (acupoints). The approach has been controversial since claims of rapid results with a wide range of clinical conditions made their way into mainstream media in the 1980s, particularly via books (*Five Minute Phobia Cure*, Callahan, 1985), radio programs (recounted in Callahan & Trubo, 2002), and newspaper and magazine articles. With its strange-looking procedures (e.g., tapping on the back of one's hand while humming a tune) and stranger explanatory models (often based on speculations that seemed totally disconnected from Western science), energy psychology quickly earned its place among clinical developments that evoke intense skepticism in mental health professionals. A Delphi poll found that most psychologists did not view energy psychology as a viable treatment option (Norcross, Koocher, & Garofalo, 2006), and the approach has been denigrated in prestigious clinical journals as resembling a pseudoscience whose proponents have presented no more than "a disjointed series of unsubstantiated assertions, ill-defined neologisms, and far-fetched case reports that blur boundaries between farce and expository prose" (Kline, 2001, p. 1188).

Bakker's Approach

An account by Bakker (2013) is the most recent peer-reviewed critique to "qualify the field of 'energy psychology' as a pseudoscience," noting that "the prefix 'pseudo-' has the meaning 'pretended'" (p. 6). Bakker points out that some 500 "psychotherapeutic models have been advanced in the literature [and] the majority persist, despite lack of supportive evidence" (p. 1). Energy psychology not only persists; it is becoming more widely used in clinical settings as well as outside the mental health profession. Since the 2006 Delphi poll, acceptance by psychotherapists has grown substantially. A 2012 paper that was generally quite critical of energy psychology and related approaches reported that a survey of 149 licensed psychotherapists—recruited from listservs such as the Association of Behavioral and Cognitive Therapies, Acceptance and Commitment Therapy, and the Society for a Science of Clinical Psychology—showed that 42.3% frequently used or were inclined to utilize "energy meridian techniques," which are based on stimulating acupoints (Gaudiano, Brown, & Miller, 2012). Use of energy psychology on a self-help basis is also increasing. More than two million people have downloaded an instruction manual for Emotional Freedom Techniques (EFT), the most popular form of energy psychology, and a Google Analytics review showed that in a sample month (June 2013), there were 9,143,000 searches worldwide for "EFT tapping" and related terms (Church, 2013).

Bakker raises a vital question. Is energy psychology another approach that, after gaining wide popular appeal, will later be discredited and shown to have misled the public, following in the steps of phrenology and mesmerism? His paper is a scholarly attempt to answer that question. It critically examines clinical and research data that would appear to support energy psychology, and it calls attention to some of the most controversial of the explanatory models that have appeared in the literature.

Framed as a "status report," the paper selects some of the weakest links in the literature and brings prodigious critical analysis to them while neglecting to examine the preponderance of evidence that supports claims of efficacy. Explanatory models that ground the approach in established psychological and neurological principles (discussion to follow) are altogether omitted, and the most promising studies are dismissed with no or minimal analysis. This pattern begins before specific studies are reviewed. The reader is informed that in 1999 "the American Psychological Association's Continuing Professional Education Committee ruled TFT [Thought Field Therapy, the original form of energy psychology] an inappropriate subject for continuing education, due to the absence of any scientific support" (Bakker, 2013, p. 3). Bakker does not mention the much more pertinent development that in November 2012 the same APA committee reversed this ruling. After exhaustive hearings over several years, the committee accepted the Association for Comprehensive Energy Psychology, whose course offerings are all related to energy psychology, as an APA continuing education sponsor (Association for Comprehensive Energy Psychology, 2012). Scientific support for the efficacy of the method had accumulated to the point that energy psychology courses met the standards for APA continuing education credit. Energy psychology courses also qualify for continuing education credit with other professional organizations, including the American Medical Association, the American Board of Family Medicine, and the American Nurses Credentialing Commission.

Much of the research support leading to these determinations is summarized in two papers I authored, both of which were published in APA journals (Feinstein, 2008, 2012), and these papers are the focus of many of Bakker's criticisms. For instance, in discussing a study using energy psychology for weight management, Bakker comes to the conclusion that "Feinstein (2012) falsely reported 'Outcomes held at one year along with reduced body mass'" (Bakker, 2013, p. 6). However, this was exactly the study's finding (Stapleton, Sheldon, & Porter, 2012). Bakker's entire analysis of that study is based on an earlier paper by the researchers published before their 1-year follow-up investigation was completed (Stapleton, Sheldon, Porter, & Whitty, 2011), a paper I did not even cite but that is nonetheless used to attempt to discredit my review.

While the inaccurate assertion that I falsely reported the study's follow-up findings may well have been an innocent error, the reader is also told about my "inability to grasp the meaning of placebo controls," my having "failed to grasp the true meaning of a dismantling study," my conclusions based on "sparse and methodologically weak evidence," my "overly optimistic" claims, and my "selectivity" in reporting the relevant literature.

Placebo Controls

Placebo control is a pivotal issue in interpreting efficacy claims for energy psychology. Are the reported clinical improvements based on active ingredients unique to the approach or are they based on nonspecific factors such as placebo, expectancy, social demand, or allegiance effects or on previously established procedures that are components of the therapy being examined? My alleged "inability to grasp the meaning of placebo controls" is based in part on my having countered the stated conclusions of the authors of two studies that attempted to distinguish active ingredient versus placebo effects. These studies investigated acupuncture point (acupoint) tapping protocols as used in TFT (Pignotti, 2005) and EFT (Waite & Holder, 2003), respectively, comparing them with sham protocols. Bakker quotes my statements in a published rejoinder (Feinstein, 2009) to two vehement critiques (McCaslin, 2009; Pignotti & Thyer, 2009) of my review of the preliminary evidence bearing upon the efficacy of energy psychology (Feinstein, 2008).

In explaining my dismissal of Pignotti's (2005) conclusions, Bakker correctly notes that I stated, "Strict adherence to the original tapping protocols is considered by most practitioners to be unnecessary." TFT, as originally formulated by Callahan, did have strict procedural guidelines, specifying not only the acupoints that needed to be tapped when treating a particular psychological condition but also the order in which they needed to be tapped (Callahan & Callahan, 1996). EFT, developed by one of Callahan's students, Gary Craig, simplified the procedures, eliminating many features, including adherence to a strictly specified order (Craig, 2011). EFT is now far more widely practiced than TFT, and the EFT studies demonstrating efficacy outnumber those of TFT. Pignotti's investigation, conducted during a TFT training class, demonstrated that the order by which acupoints were tapped did not impact the outcome, a principle that is widely understood among energy psychology practitioners, which is the point I was making. Pignotti, however, interpreted this finding as invalidating the TFT protocols, an interpretation that has been echoed by subsequent detractors of energy psychology (e.g., Lohr, Olatunji, & Devilly, 2008; Gaudiano et al., 2012). Not adequately explained in these discussions is Pignotti's concurrent finding that 64 of the 66 participants reported that their subjective emotional distress had been eliminated after the tapping. If that success rate in reducing emotional distress could be produced by placebo, expectation, social demand, or expectancy, active ingredients that are limited to specific therapies would be superfluous. The inability to grasp the meaning of placebo controls extends to overestimating as well as underestimating the power of placebo and other nonspecific effects.

The other statement that alerted Bakker to my "inability to grasp the meaning of placebo controls" was my contention that the data from the Pignotti (2005) and Waite and Holder (2003) studies indeed "support the efficacy of tapping while activating an emotional concern." Bakker presents this as a naïve statement, but in the paper being quoted (Feinstein, 2009), I went on to discuss assumptions that skew the interpretation of data in order to dismiss findings that do not conform to prevailing paradigms (Kuhn, 1996):

> For instance, assuming that the *possibility* of extraneous influences in an experiment *explains* unexpected findings is a way of discounting anomalous observations. Pignotti (2005) observed a 97% success rate for two variations of tapping. Waite and Holder (2003) reported .001, .001, and .003 pre/post improvement probabilities in three variations of tapping. ... While it is possible that these findings could be explained by non-specific therapeutic factors, a more parsimonious (though outside-the-paradigm) conclusion would be that percussion using the fingers while mentally activating a fearful stimulus or other emotional problem, even during a single brief session, reduces arousal to the stimulus. Parsimony involves not only striving for the simplest available explanations in interpreting data; it also requires that the explanations used reasonably account for all the data. (Feinstein, 2009, pp. 266–267).

In brief, pointing to the possibility that placebo effects *could be* involved in a therapy's success does not nullify outcome data. It highlights unanswered questions that need to be resolved. Bakker prudently suggests that dismantling studies are a way of addressing this issue. However, despite his claim that, in my 2012 review, I failed to "grasp the true meaning of a dismantling study" (Bakker, 2013, p. 6), that same paper emphasized that "dismantling studies … are needed to identify the active ingredients in energy psychology protocols," and that they could also answer numerous additional questions that "would guide clinicians" in developing more effective treatment strategies (Feinstein, 2012, p. 375). Assigning observed improvements of an unconventional therapy to placebo or other nonspecific effects until proven otherwise is no more scientifically sound for interpreting outcome data than not allowing for the possibility.

The Preponderance of Evidence

Bakker recognizes APA Division 12 for developing criteria that attempt to "sort the wheat from the chaff" in evaluating evidence bearing upon the efficacy of a given psychotherapy (Bakker, 2013, p. 1). He then goes on to criticize a conclusion of my 2008 paper that energy psychology protocols have passed "the threshold formulated by Division 12" as being "probably efficacious" in treating two specified conditions. His stated objection is that this conclusion was based on "sparse and methodologically weak evidence" (p. 4). While I was reporting my own analysis, clearly noting that "Division 12 has not yet evaluated either study" (2009, p. 210), none of the critics of the 2008 paper have identified a fallacy in the argument that the studies meet the Division 12 criteria in use at the time.

Bakker, however, goes further, holding the studies reviewed in my 2012 paper to a different standard than the Division 12 criteria, which, incidentally, have considerable overlap with FDA standards for clinical trials (Food and Drug Administration, 1998) in the dimensions Bakker assails. For instance, the standards Bakker seems to impose on research for it to lend evidence of efficacy he considers credible discount studies that use wait-list controls as well as virtually all the other comparison conditions used in my sample, noting derisively that none of the investigations "employed a sham procedure control or were dismantling studies." There is no argument that robust studies would be useful for more clearly delineating the role, in energy psychology outcomes, of nonspecific therapeutic factors and active ingredients not common to other therapies. Although a recent dismantling study comparing all the components of EFT with a protocol that substituted acupoint tapping with diaphragmatic breathing did show that acupoint tapping is an active ingredient (Fox, 2013), the existing research, as I noted in the 2012 paper, still "represents a relatively early stage in efforts to establish the efficacy of energy psychology protocols" (p. 373). The appropriate argument, however, is not whether the current research unambiguously establishes efficacy for energy psychology interventions. Rather, it is whether readers of this journal should be discouraged from learning more about the approach ("clinicians have not been offered any justification to stray into energy psychology techniques"; Bakker, 2013, p. 6) or encouraged to explore it because the existing research shows promise that acupoint simulation may be "a technique that can be used with confidence for quickly altering the neural pathways that underlie psychological problems" (Feinstein, 2012, p. 377).

Bakker finds it "surprising" that "despite criticisms of existing studies … Feinstein (2012) once more completed a review of such therapies that did not recognize the problems in the field" (p. 5). He goes so far, in fact, as to suggest: "Further research is highly unlikely to be scientifically productive, and scientist practitioners are advised to continue to adhere to well-established cognitive and behavioural principles" (p. 1). He does not mention that of the 51 peer-reviewed studies or clinical reports that met the search criteria of the review he was critiquing (with 39 of them having been published after the 2008 review), all 51 described positive outcomes (Feinstein, 2012). Granted, as discussed previously, interpretations of the meaning of the positive clinical effects reported by Pignotti (2005) and Waite and Holder (2003) are debatable, but both studies described significant improvement after a brief tapping session. All 51 reports were, in fact, uncannily consistent in showing improvement following the energy psychology treatment.

The 2012 review used the following search criteria: "articles had to a) examine the use of acupoint tapping (the most widely used form of acupoint stimulation by energy psychology practitioners) within a psychotherapeutic or coaching framework, b) present clinical outcomes, and c) have been peer-reviewed" (p. 365). More than 3,000 entries in the psychological and acupuncture literature were brought up by the search terms that were used, with 51 papers meeting these criteria (most acupuncture studies investigate the treatment of physical conditions outside of psychotherapeutic frameworks). Since the purpose of this response to Bakker's critique is to establish what can be concluded with confidence from the studies I reviewed and to acknowledge where the existing evidence is weak, it provides an opportunity to correct an omission from my 2012 review. It has been brought to my attention that I overlooked an Internet-only study conducted in Germany in which 70 participants who met the criteria for obsessive-compulsive disorder (OCD) based on online inventories were randomly assigned to an acupoint tapping or a progressive relaxation treatment. They were provided with online manuals and video demonstrations. The tapping group reported being more likely to continue to use the method (72%) than did the relaxation group (48%), and modest symptom reduction was found on standardized inventories but not on the primary OCD-specific inventory (Moritz et al., 2011). OCD generally has a high rate of treatment failure (Moritz et al., 2011), and it could be argued that a self-help approach with no individualized instruction or live therapist contact over a 4-week period was not an adequate test of acupoint tapping for this condition. Nonetheless, not including the study was a significant omission because it annuls the claim that 100% of the papers in my sample reported substantial improvements on targeted conditions.

Of the 51 reports that were identified, 18 randomized controlled trials (RCTs) that utilized standardized measures were analyzed. The Pignotti (2005) and Waite and Holder (2003) studies were not included in this group because their only outcome measures were in-the-moment verbal reports of subjective distress. As Bakker points out, I mistakenly noted that the four controlled studies that were not counted as RCTs were all excluded because they were not fully randomized, another error I deeply regret. While two of the controlled studies were, indeed, not randomized, Pignotti (2005) and Waite and Holder (2003) were not included because they did not use validated and reliable outcome measures (Waite & Holder also did not attempt to maintain fidelity to the EFT manual). The 18 RCTs that were analyzed all used such measures, with nine relying entirely on self-inventories and the other nine adding to self-inventories external or objective pre/post measures, such as structured clinician-administered diagnostic interviews or observed avoidance of a feared stimulus in the laboratory setting. The 18 RCTs were reviewed on dimensions such as the use of objective versus exclusively subjective measures, the use of blinding, statistical considerations, and the use of follow-up investigation, leading to the conclusion: "These studies have consistently demonstrated strong effect sizes and other positive statistical results that far exceed chance after relatively few treatment sessions" (p. 377).

Unusual Speed and Success Rates

Bakker devotes more space to his critique of an investigation of the ability of EFT to reduce food cravings than to any of the other studies in my two reviews. Ninety-six participants were randomized into a wait-list group and a treatment group that participated in four 2-hour group EFT sessions over a 4-week period (Stapleton et al., 2011; with a follow-up report published in 2012). Significant improvements were found post-treatment in a) food cravings, b) the ability to restrain from food cravings, c) the subjective power of food, and d) general measures of psychological coping. Averages for weight and body mass index (BMI) had decreased by the end of the program, but not significantly. On 6-month follow-up, the reduced cravings held, along with other subjective gains. Weight and BMI continued to decrease and reached statistical significance ($p < .05$) by the time of the 12-month assessments (Stapleton et al., 2012). Stapleton et al. not only demonstrated that EFT was effective in weight reduction, they also illustrated how psychological changes early in a weight management program can be precursors to significant reductions in weight and BMI. Objective changes followed subjective changes and appear to have been causally related to them. Obesity is among the most serious and prevalent health problems that psychotherapists can impact (Shaw, O'Rourke, Del Mar, & Kenardy, 2005), and a more balanced review might have acknowledged the study's contributions to this important line of investigation. Instead, Bakker's comments were limited primarily to the same objections to the energy psychology research data he repeated throughout his paper: It is *possible* that the positive results were due to factors that are not unique to EFT.

This is certainly a question that needs to be resolved and, as Bakker and I agree, more robust dismantling studies are needed to fully resolve it. However, calling for additional comparison and dismantling studies is not the only path for drawing rational conclusions from a body of evidence about a clinical approach. While Bakker's stated objections to existing studies kept coming back to the question of controlling for nonspecific effects and components shared with established therapies, he ignored much of the more salient literature. For instance, in four studies, a *single* energy psychology session resulted in significant improvements in PTSD (Church, Piña, Reategui, & Brooks, 2011; Connolly, Roe-Sepowitz, Sakai, & Edwards, 2013; Connolly & Sakai, 2011; Sakai, Connolly, & Oas, 2010). In one of these single-session studies, 47 of 50 orphaned survivors of genocide all went from above to below PTSD thresholds on a standardized inventory completed by their caregivers (Sakai et al., 2010). The gains persisted on 1-year follow-up. In a study of 49 veterans with PTSD, 86% went from above to below PTSD thresholds after six sessions (Church et al., 2013, available online at the time of the 2012 review).

In comparison, in Cognitive Behavioral Therapy (CBT) studies, about half of PTSD clients are nonresponsive (Kar, 2011), and 8 to 12 sessions are generally required when treatment is successful (Bisson et al., 2007). Even in an energy psychology PTSD study that Bakker disparaged (Karatzias et al., 2011) because of his objections to the comparison treatment, Eye Movement Desensitization and Reprocessing (EMDR), treatment times were much briefer. Conducted by Scotland's National Health Service, clients in this well-designed study were allowed as many as eight treatment sessions of up to an hour each. They needed, however, on average, only 3.8 sessions (energy psychology) and 3.7 sessions (EMDR) to complete the therapy, having attained highly significant ($p < .001$) pre/post-treatment improvements with large effect sizes. While a flaw in this study was the high dropout rate (approximately 40%), those who benefitted overcame their PTSD in an average of less than four sessions. The dropout rates in most of the studies in my sample were, incidentally, much lower than in the Karatzias et al. study, and they were also low in comparison with the dropout rates found in studies of CBT treatments for PTSD (Schottenbauer, Glass, Arnkoff, Tendick, & Gray, 2008).

While these findings are preliminary, and my review called for "head-to-head clinical trials with other established treatments" (Feinstein, 2012, p. 375), the findings are highly relevant for a paper titled "The Current Status of Energy Psychology" (Bakker, 2013). If the speed and success rates following acupoint stimulation are due to nonspecific effects and established treatment components, why do the preliminary studies frequently show that energy psychology protocols outperform the speed and success rates of CBT found in the systematic reviews cited above? Some light on this question is shed by a comparison study treating earthquake survivors suffering with PTSD. Ninety-one subjects were randomly assigned to CBT treatment alone or CBT treatment combined with acupoint stimulation (Zhang, Feng, Xie, Xu, & Chen, 2011). Participants in both groups improved, but the improvement for those receiving the acupoint treatment was significantly stronger ($p < .01$) than the improvement for those who received CBT alone. While the investigators did not use a standard energy psychology protocol, the study controls for nonspecific therapeutic effects and it shows acupoint stimulation (in this case using an electronic acupoint stimulator instead of tapping) to be an active ingredient that improved outcomes when combined with CBT.

Active Ingredients That Are Unique to Energy Psychology

The unique, shared component of most energy psychology protocols is the stimulation of acupoints. It can be inferred from the aforementioned studies and others in my sample that this is an active component that leads to strong therapeutic effects, but more direct scientific evidence is also available. A research program at Harvard Medical School investigating the effects of stimulating specific acupuncture points has been using fMRIs, PET scans, and other imaging techniques for more than a decade (Fang et al., 2009; Hui et al., 2000). They have consistently found that the stimulation of certain points with needles reliably produces prominent decreases of activity in limbic areas associated with fear and other threat-based emotions. Various studies suggest an equivalency between the clinical effects of acupuncture with needles and acupoint stimulation based on physical pressure (e.g., Takakura & Yajima, 2009). While imaging studies of the effects of acupoint tapping during energy psychology protocols would be informative, three studies using electrical measures of brain activity with tapping subjects (Diepold & Goldstein, 2009; Lambrou, Pratt, & Chevalier, 2003; Swingle, Pulos, & Swingle, 2004) are consistent with the interpretation that the active ingredient is the stimulation of the acupoints, whether by tapping or other methods.

One of the reasons Bakker judges energy psychology to be "pseudoscientific" is that he finds it to have "an unsupported and implausible theoretical basis" (p. 1). Energy psychology actually has two literatures that attempt to establish a theoretical basis. One draws its explanatory models from ancient healing and spiritual traditions, using terms that Bakker points to as examples of unsupported concepts, such as "meridians," "energy fields," and "energy blockages" (p. 3). But even these concepts are beginning to find empirical support. Meridian pathways that correspond with the ancient Chinese maps have been shown to travel along the body's connective tissue (Langevin & Yandow, 2002). Scientists speak of energy fields as "biofields" that regulate various body functions (Rubik, 2002). For instance, Thomas Insel, the director of the U.S. National Institute of Mental Health, recently pointed to accumulating evidence that the synchronization of "large scale electrical oscillations across distant brain regions" allows content-specific information to be transmitted (National Institute of Mental Health, 2012, p. 1).

The "other" literature—which Bakker does not cite—attempts to reconcile acupoint tapping with more established psychological concepts without relying on constructs that cannot be detected or measured (Feinstein, 2010; Lane, 2009; Ruden, 2005, 2010). For instance, with its imaginal activation of troubling scenes, energy psychology is clearly an exposure technique. But simultaneous with that exposure, signals are sent that rapidly deactivate arousal in the amygdala and other limbic structures (Fang et al., 2009; Hui et al., 2000). Energy psychology *is* an exposure technique, but it *adds* a component that makes exposure quicker and more potent.

Single-session cures of any long-standing psychological problem are suspect to seasoned psychotherapists, yet reports of significant, measurable improvement appear with surprising frequency in formal studies as well as clinical reports. I have interviewed the principal investigators of each of the four PTSD studies reporting strong symptom relief after a single session. In no case did they feel that a single session is adequate. They believed that additional sessions would have been beneficial to many of their participants but felt compelled to use a single-session design due to practical constraints. Still, the amygdala deactivation model begins to explain the rapid results that were attained in all four studies. A traumatic memory or trigger is brought to mind, the limbic system is aroused, and the acupoint tapping sends signals to the brain that turn off the threat response until the person is able to focus on the memory or trigger with no physiological arousal. This experience of safety in the imagined presence of the formerly threat-inducing memory or trigger is integrated and becomes a new learned response. Concomitant physiological changes include increased prefrontal activity and decreased cortisol levels as the stress response is deactivated. Church, Yount, and Brooks (2012) found, for instance, that a single tapping session was not only more effective than a standard supportive counseling session in reducing self-reported distress, the treatment sharply reduced cortisol levels. Elevated cortisol levels are associated with psychological conditions such as depression and anxiety as well as many organic diseases. Cortisol levels were not similarly reduced in control subjects who received supportive counseling or no treatment.

Other ways of describing energy psychology treatments in terms that are familiar to the mental health community are also emerging. Among the most promising in relation to establishing a more credible theoretical basis for the approach is the way acupoint tapping simultaneous with the mental activation of irrational fear and other problematic emotions seems to utilize the principles of memory reconsolidation (Ecker, Ticic, & Hulley, 2012) to depotentiate neural pathways and produce rapid changes in deeply embedded beliefs and emotional patterns (Feinstein, 2013).

Conclusion

As the popularity of energy psychology continues to grow, psychologists who are convinced that the public is being deceived are understandably alarmed. Energy psychology made a very bad initial impression with the mental health community, and the research that might counter that impression has only started to accumulate in the past few years. Gary Bakker does the field a service by taking a critical look at the claims of energy psychology proponents and analyzing with a skeptical eye the research that purportedly backs those claims. This paper has attempted to address each of his major concerns and to demonstrate that evidence backing three decades of extraordinary claims about energy psychology's speed and success rates is finally appearing.

References

Association for Comprehensive Energy Psychology. (2012). APA approves ACEP to provide CE credits for psychologists. Retrieved October 12, 2013 from http://energypsych.org/displaycommon.cfm?an=1&subarticlenbr=329

Bakker, G. M. (2013, November). The current status of energy psychology: Extraordinary claims with less than ordinary evidence. *Clinical Psychologist, 17*(3), 91–99. Article first published online, July 30, 2013. doi:10.1111/cp.12020

Bisson, J. I., Ehlers, A., Matthews, R., Pilling, S., Richards, D., & Turner, S. (2007). Psychological treatments for chronic post-traumatic stress disorder: Systematic review and meta-analysis. *British Journal of Psychiatry, 190*, 97–104. doi:10.1192/bjp.bp.106.021402

Callahan, R. (1985). *Five minute phobia cure.* Wilmington, DE: Enterprise.

Callahan, R. J., & Callahan, J. (1996). *Thought Field Therapy (TFT) and trauma: Treatment and theory.* Indian Wells, CA: Thought Field Therapy Training Center.

Callahan, R. J., & Trubo, R. (2002). *Tapping the healer within.* New York, NY: McGraw-Hill.

Church, D. (2013). Clinical EFT as an evidence-based practice for the treatment of psychological and physiological conditions. *Psychology, 4*, 645–654. doi:10.4236/psych.2013.48092

Church, D., Hawk, C., Brooks, A., Toukolehto, O., Wren, M., Dinter, I., & Stein, P. (2013). Psychological trauma in veterans using EFT (Emotional Freedom Techniques): A randomized controlled trial. *Journal of Nervous and Mental Disease, 201*, 153–160. doi:10.1097/NMD.0b013e31827f6351

Church, D., Piña, O., Reategui, C., & Brooks, A. (2011). Single session reduction of the intensity of traumatic memories in abused adolescents after EFT: A randomized controlled pilot study. *Traumatology, 18*(3), 73–79. doi:10.1177/1534765611426788

Church, D., Yount, G., & Brooks, A. (2012). The effect of Emotional Freedom Techniques (EFT) on stress biochemistry: A randomized controlled trial. *Journal of Nervous and Mental Disease, 200*, 891–896. doi:10.1097/NMD.0b013e31826b9fc1

Connolly, S., Roe-Sepowitz, D., Sakai, C., & Edwards, J. (2013). Utilizing community resources to treat PTSD: A randomized controlled study using Thought Field Therapy. *African Journal of Traumatic Stress, 3*(1), 24–32.

Connolly, S., & Sakai, C. (2011). Brief trauma intervention with Rwandan genocide survivors using Thought Field Therapy. *International Journal of Emergency Mental Health, 13*(3), 161–172.

Craig, G. (2011). *The EFT manual* (2nd ed.). Santa Rosa, CA: Energy Psychology Press.

Diepold, J. H., & Goldstein, D. (2009). Thought field therapy and QEEG changes in the treatment of trauma: A case study. *Traumatology, 15*, 85–93. doi:10.1177/1534765608325304

Ecker, B., Ticic, R., & Hulley, L. (2012). *Unlocking the emotional brain: Eliminating symptoms at their roots using memory reconsolidation.* New York, NY: Routledge.

Fang, J., Jin, Z., Wang, Y., Li, K., Kong, J., Nixon, E. E., … Hui, K. K.-S. (2009). The salient characteristics of the central effects of acupuncture needling: Limbic-paralimbic-neocortical network modulation. *Human Brain Mapping, 30*, 1196–1206. doi:10.1002/hbm.20583

Feinstein, D. (2008). Energy psychology: A review of the preliminary evidence. *Psychotherapy: Theory, Research, Practice, Training, 45*(2), 199–213. doi:10.1037/0033-3204.45.2.199

Feinstein, D. (2009). Facts, paradigms, and anomalies in the acceptance of energy psychology: A rejoinder to McCaslin's (2009) and Pignotti and Thyer's (2009) comments on Feinstein (2008a). *Psychotherapy: Theory, Research, Practice, Training, 46*(2), 262–269. doi:10.1037/a0016086

Feinstein, D. (2010). Rapid treatment of PTSD: Why psychological exposure with acupoint tapping may be effective. *Psychotherapy: Theory, Research, Practice, Training, 47*(3), 385–402. doi:10.1037/a0021171

Feinstein, D. (2012). Acupoint stimulation in treating psychological disorders: Evidence of efficacy. *Review of General Psychology, 16*(4), 364–380. doi:10.1037/a0028602

Feinstein, D. (2013). Memory reconsolidation and energy psychology. Retrieved from http://reconsolidation.EnergyPsychEd.com

Food and Drug Administration. (1998). *Guidance for industry: Providing clinical evidence of effectiveness for human drug and biological products.* Rockville, MD: U.S. Department of Health and Human Services.

Fox, L. (2013). Is acupoint tapping an active ingredient or an inert placebo in Emotional Freedom Techniques (EFT)? A randomized controlled dismantling study. *Energy Psychology: Theory, Research, and Treatment, 5*(2), 15–28.

Gaudiano, B. A., Brown, L. A., & Miller, I. W. (2012). Tapping their patients' problems away? Characteristics of psychotherapists using energy meridian techniques. *Research on Social Work Practice, 22*, 647–655. doi:10.1177/1049731512448468

Hui, K. K. S, Liu, J., Makris, N., Gollub, R. W., Chen, A. J. W., Moore, C. I., … Kwong, K. K. (2000). Acupuncture modulates the limbic system and subcortical gray structures of the human brain: Evidence from fMRI studies in normal subjects. *Human Brain Mapping, 9*, 13–25. doi:10.1002/(SICI)1097-0193(2000)9:1<13::AID-HBM2>3.0.CO;2-F

Kar, N. (2011). Cognitive behavioral therapy for the treatment of post-traumatic stress disorder: A review. *Neuropsychiatric Disease and Treatment, 7*, 167–181. doi:10.2147/NDT.S10389

Karatzias, T., Power, K., Brown, K., McGoldrick, T., Begum, M., Young, J., … Adams, S. (2011). A controlled comparison of the effectiveness and efficiency of two psychological therapies for posttraumatic stress disorder: Eye Movement Desensitization and Reprocessing vs. Emotional Freedom Techniques. *Journal of Nervous and Mental Diseases, 199*, 372–378. doi:10.1097/MND.0b013e31821cd26

Kline, J. P. (2001). Heart Rate Variability does not tap putative efficacy of Thought Field Therapy. *Journal of Clinical Psychology, 57*, 1187–1192.

Kuhn, T. S. (1996). *The structure of scientific revolutions* (3rd ed.). Chicago, IL: University of Chicago Press.

Lambrou, P. T., Pratt, G. J., & Chevalier, G. (2003). Physiological and psychological effects of a mind/body therapy on claustrophobia. *Subtle Energies and Energy Medicine, 14*, 239–251.

Lane, J. (2009). The neurochemistry of counterconditioning: Acupressure desensitization in psychotherapy. *Energy Psychology: Theory, Research, and Treatment, 1*(1), 31–44. doi:10.9769.2009.1.1.JRL

Langevin H.M., & Yandow J.A. (2002). Relationship of acupuncture points and meridians to connective tissue planes. *Anatomical Record, 269*, 257–265. doi:10.1002/ar.10185

Lohr, J. M., Olatunji, B. O., & Devilly, G. J. (2008). Threats to evidence-based treatment of trauma: Professional issues and implications. *International Review of* Victimology, *15*, 123–146. doi:10.1177/026975800801500204

McCaslin, D. (2009). A review of efficacy claims in energy psychology. *Psychotherapy: Research, Practice, Training, 46*, 249–256. doi:10.1037/a0016025

Moritz, S., Aravena, S. C., Guczka, S. R., Schilling, L., Eichenberg, C., Raubart, G., ... Jelinek, L. (2011). Knock, and it will be opened to you? An evaluation of meridian-tapping in obsessive-compulsive disorder (OCD). *Journal of Behavior Therapy and Experimental Psychiatry, 42*(1), 81–88. doi:10.1016/j.jbtep.2010.07.002

National Institute of Mental Health. (2012, November 1). Insynch brain waves hold memory of object just seen [Press release]. Retrieved from http://www.nimh.nih.gov/science-news/2012/in-sync-brain-waves-hold-memory-of-objects-just-seen.shtml

Norcross, J. C., Koocher, G. P., & Garofalo, G. P. (2006). Discredited psychological treatments and tests: A Delphi poll. *Professional Psychology: Research and Practice, 37*, 515–522. doi:10.1037/0735-7028.37.5.515

Pignotti, M. (2005). Thought Field Therapy Voice Technology vs. random meridian point sequences: A single-blind controlled experiment. *Scientific Review of Mental Health Practice, 4*(1), 72–81.

Pignotti, M., & Thyer, B. (2009). Some comments on "Energy Psychology: A Review of the Evidence": Premature conclusions based on incomplete evidence? *Psychotherapy: Research, Practice, Training, 46*, 257–261. doi:10.1037/a0016027

Rubik, B. (2002). The biofield hypothesis: Its biophysical basis and role in medicine. *Journal of Alternative and Complementary Medicine, 8*, 703–717.

Ruden, R. A. (2005). A neurological basis for the observed peripheral sensory modulation of emotional responses. *Traumatology, 11*, 145–158. doi:10.1177/153476560501100301

Ruden, R. A. (2010). *When the past is always present: Emotional traumatization, causes, and cures.* New York, NY: Routledge.

Sakai, C. S., Connolly, S. M., & Oas, P. (2010). Treatment of PTSD in Rwandan genocide survivors using Thought Field Therapy. *International Journal of Emergency Mental Health, 12*(1), 41–50.

Schottenbauer, M. A., Glass, C. R., Arnkoff, D. B., Tendick, V., & Gray S. H. (2008). Nonresponse and dropout rates in outcome studies on PTSD: Review and methodological considerations. *Psychiatry, 71*, 134–168. doi:10.1521/psyc.2008.71.2.134

Shaw, K., O'Rourke, P., Del Mar, C., & Kenardy, J. (2005). Psychological interventions for overweight or obesity. *Cochrane Database of Systematic Reviews, 2005*, Issue 2. Art. No.: CD003818.

Stapleton, P., Sheldon, T., & Porter, B. (2012). Clinical benefits of Emotional Freedom Techniques on food cravings 12-months follow-up: A randomized controlled trial. *Energy Psychology: Theory, Research, and Treatment, 4*(1), 13–24. doi:10.9769.EPJ.2012.4.1.PS

Stapleton, P., Sheldon, T., Porter, B., & Whitty, J. (2011). A randomised clinical trial of a meridian-based intervention for food cravings with six-month follow-up. *Behaviour Change, 28*(1), 1–16. doi:10.1375/bech.28.1.1

Swingle, P. G., Pulos, L., & Swingle, M. K. (2004). Neurophysiological indicators of EFT treatment of posttraumatic stress. *Subtle Energies and Energy Medicine, 15*, 75–86.

Takakura, N., & Yajima, H. (2009). Analgesic effect of acupuncture needle penetration: A double-blind crossover study. *Open Medicine, 3*(2). Retrieved October 13, 2013, from http://www.openmedicine.ca/article/view/189/235

Waite, L. W., & Holder, M. D. (2003). Assessment of the emotional freedom technique: An alternative treatment for fear. *Scientific Review of Mental Health Practice, 2*(1), 20–26.

Wells, S., Polglase, K., Andrews, H. B., Carrington, P., & Baker, A. H. (2003). Evaluation of a meridian-based intervention, emotional freedom techniques (EFT), for reducing specific phobias of small animals. *Journal of Clinical Psychology, 59*, 943–966. doi:10.1002/jclp.10189

Zhang, Y., Feng, B., Xie, J. P., Xu, F. Z., & Chen, J. (2011). Clinical study on treatment of the earthquake-caused post-traumatic stress disorder by cognitive-behavior therapy and acupoint stimulation. *Journal of Traditional Chinese Medicine, 31*, 60–63. doi:10.1016/S0254-6272(11)60014-9

REVIEW ARTICLE

A Bigger Swamp Is Still a Swamp: Comments on Feinstein (2014)

Gary M. Bakker, School of Medicine, University of Tasmania

Correspondence: Gary M. Bakker, School of Medicine, University of Tasmania, PO Box 1495, Launceston, Tasmania 7250, Australia. Email: gary.bakker@bigpond.com

David Feinstein's response, "Comment on 'The current status of energy psychology': Growing evidence for extraordinary claims" (2014a) to my review "The current status of energy psychology: Extraordinary claims with less than ordinary evidence" (Bakker, 2013) claims to demonstrate that my selection and reporting of studies skews my data, and that (a) scientific support for the efficacy of energy psychology is accumulating, (b) initial findings suggest that the method is surprisingly rapid and effective, and (c) plausible mechanisms are consistent with established psychological principles.

On the contrary, my review illustrated how inappropriately skewed Feinstein's (2008, 2012) citation of studies has been, (a) the support for energy psychology's efficacy has flat-lined; (b) if something is surprisingly rapid and effective, it is not energy psychology; and (c) "tapping on meridians" and "energy fields" are still not consistent with established psychological principles.

The data I have "skewed" toward are studies with controls that add to our theoretical base (such as dismantling studies) by seeking out *what* is working. Thousands of wait-list control studies since Hawthorne have shown us that almost anything "works." "Most psychotherapies can be shown to be statistically superior to no treatment" (Herbert & Gaudiano, 2005, p. 899) due to the known powerful influences of expectancy, the therapeutic relationship, hope, and treatment credibility. Randomized controlled trials (RCTs) with wait-list controls are theoretically almost valueless. David and Montgomery (2011) have described how a "pseudoscientific"/"junk-science" intervention based on any "voodoo" theory can claim empirical validation if supported by an RCT with a wait-list control, which really only shows it can be an effective placebo treatment.

But energy psychology techniques also contain known-effective elements, especially imaginal exposure. Rosen and Davison (2003) have described techniques that add arbitrary elements to procedures that we know can make a difference as "purple hat therapies."

> Hypothetically, a doctor could ask clients with driving phobias to wear a large purple hat while applying relaxation and cognitive coping skills to in vivo practice. The practitioner places a band of magnets in the purple hats, claiming that particular algorithms for positioning the magnets are determined by age, sex, and personality structure of the client. When properly placed, so the practitioner claims, magnets reorient energy fields, accelerate information processing, improve interhemispheric coherence, and eliminate phobic avoidance. The inventor might call his method "purple hat therapy" (PHT) or "electro Magnetic Desensitization and Remobilization" (eMDR), conduct a single RCT against no treatment, and apply for listing as an EST. (Rosen & Davison, 2003, pp. 304–305).

A redundant elaboration on a known-to-be-effective therapy, such as exposure therapy, is not a new therapy, and provides no support for its putative underlying theory. We need to find out what *about* EFT works. Is it the big sell that generally accompanies it? Or the embedded concurrent exposure therapy? Or the tapping? On a meridian? On a certain acupoint? Different points for different problems? To assert that "EFT works," it is necessary to show that (a) it works, *and* (b) that it is *the EFT* working.

Feinstein's reviews (2008, 2012) cited masses of anecdotal reports, case studies, "systematic observations," uncontrolled outcome studies, and randomized controlled trials using wait-list controls or benign comparisons such as "supportive interviews" or "diaphragmatic breathing." None of these tell us whether it is the essence of energy psychology—meridian tapping—that is working. His reviews were skewed toward atheoretical positive-results studies. He selectively omitted the only two fully controlled studies to date with a sham placebo control condition included (Pignotti, 2005; Waite & Holder, 2003), both of which produced negative results. When this was first noted, he responded citing length concerns (Feinstein, 2009). When this defence did not wash, he claimed the two studies "did not use full randomization" (2012, p. 2). Since my review pointed out they *were* adequately randomized, he now claims they did not use "standardized outcome measures" (Feinstein, 2014a), even though in his 2012 review he considered that they did. Feinstein had considered self-report of SUD (subjective units of distress) scale scores as reliable and valid as many other self-report measures.

Feinstein has been selective in his review of the data, and with shifting unjustified criteria. I have been open about, and have explained, my "skewed" examination of the available studies. He accuses my review of "neglecting to examine the preponderance of evidence that supports claims of efficacy." My review did examine it, and found it severely wanting. A greater volume of anecdotes and poorly controlled studies by devotees adds nothing to the weight of evidence. "A bigger swamp is not a lake. Clarity results from depth."

Feinstein defends his understanding of placebo controls by pointing to his acknowledgment that TFT's fussy tapping protocols have become less popular and less researched since Pignotti's (2005) finding that the other energy psychology technique, the simpler generic tapping protocols of EFT, is just as effective. But this is not what Pignotti (2005) found. His control subjects were not tapped on EFT acupoints in an EFT sequence. They tapped themselves in a random sequence on TFT acupoints. Energy psychology practitioners have not justified turning from TFT to EFT by citing Pignotti's (2005) finding. Instead it has been rejected or ignored. (It is significant to note that Callahan [1985] had 20 years to check whether the tapping locations and sequences of TFT are necessary before Pignotti's [2005] very simple study found that they are not).

So Feinstein resorted to asserting that any sequence of "tapping on the body while attuning to a problem" (Feinstein, 2009, p. 263) can be effective. But then one of Waite and Holder's (2003) equally effective conditions had subjects tapping on a doll. So now Feinstein makes conclusions about "percussion using the fingers." Not on acupoints, not on meridians, not even on one's body. What is left at the core of energy psychology techniques?

The next step, as described by Feinstein (2013), is "surrogate tapping" or "long distance healing," in which the practitioner taps on *him* or *herself* and applies other elements of energy psychology protocols as if he or she were the patient, while "holding the intention of helping that person."

The pool of psychotherapeutic options open to the indiscriminate practitioner has now moved well past the 500 mark (Eisner, 2000) with, for example, the recent addition of the Havening Techniques in which even tapping is not necessary. One can use Havening Touch, or counting backward, or eye rolling, or humming a song, or stroking, or an "ommm" on exhalation (Ruden & Ruden, 2010). Feinstein (2014b) has described the Havening Techniques as a "monumental accomplishment...where the techniques presented become the mainstays of psychology and healing."

Feinstein (2014a) claims that "pointing to the possibility that placebo effects *could be* involved in a therapy's success does not nullify outcome data." If it does not nullify them, it at the least severely weakens them, and that was my thesis as indicated in the review article's title (Bakker, 2013). The onus is on the proposer of extraordinary claims to support them, not on the skeptic to be perpetually debunking them (Lilienfeld, Lynn, & Lohr, 2003). To merely footnote that "dismantling studies...are needed" (Feinstein, 2012), but to ignore the only two undertaken to date, is inadequate.

Feinstein's (2014a) assertion that "the method is surprisingly rapid and effective" does not strengthen his position. In fact such overly optimistic claims are known to be characteristic of pseudoscientific movements. "Consistent with the characteristics of pseudoscience (Lilienfeld, 1998), EMT [energy meridian techniques] proponents often focus on confirming evidence while ignoring disconfirming research (e.g., biased literature reviews by EMT proponents), offer persuasive rhetoric in lieu of scientific evidence (e.g., claims of "rapid cures" and an emphasis on vivid clinical anecdotes)" (Gaudiano, Brown, & Miller, 2012, p. 652). Rapidity of effect is a hallmark of placebo response. All clinicians know how to interpret the report of a patient that their antidepressant began working from Day 1. Such alleged rapidity and universal efficacy should in fact make support for the specific effects of meridian tapping easier to obtain. Subtle statistical analyses should be unnecessary. This is what Pignotti (2005) found in discovering evidence *against* the protocols of TFT.

Although it is difficult to undertake fully-placebo-controlled trials with most psychotherapies (Benedetti, 2009, p. 142), energy psychology techniques are "somatic interventions" (Feinstein & Church, 2010) and therefore quite simple to develop control conditions for (Herbert & Gaudiano, 2005). In fact, subjects do not even need to know they are undergoing therapy. This makes the elaborate induction sessions "selling" the model, as described in most trials, an unnecessary, indeed a placebo/expectancy, complication.

Feinstein's (2014a) citation of a small number of weak descriptive correlational neural imaging studies merely points up the thin ice upon which energy psychology rests. For example, the very existence of meridian pathways is supported by only one study (Langevin & Yandow, 2002), which claimed to find an 80% correspondence between acupuncture points and the location of connective tissue planes in postmortem tissue sections. It did not find meridians. No one has. Other findings are said to be "consistent with" his extraordinary interpretations. They discover or establish nothing. Anatomy textbooks remain unrevised.

Feinstein (2014a) also misrepresents the growth in popularity of energy psychology among therapists. He cites Gaudiano, Brown, and Miller's (2012) "survey of 149 licensed psychotherapists," as showing "that 42.3% frequently used or were inclined to utilize 'energy meridian techniques'" (EMTs). This implies that 149 psychotherapists were approached and questioned. In fact, an advertisement was widely distributed and 149 therapists responded. This was very much not a random sampling. Respondees were self-selective. Gaudiano, Brown, and Miller (2012) themselves reference studies giving random sample rates of EMT use of 6% for EFT and 3% for TFT. Feinstein's (2014a) 42.3% figure is highly misleading. Gaudiano, Brown, and Miller (2012) go on to report that EMT users are significantly more likely to not have a doctoral degree, not be psychologists, be indiscriminately eclectic, rely on personal intuition, endorse magical beliefs about health, and score lower on a measure of critical thinking ability.

The only conclusions that can justifiably be drawn from the entire energy psychology phenomenon are:

(a) That exposure techniques work—which is already known;
(b) That nonspecific effects such as placebo, expectancy, relationship, etc. effects are important—which is already known; and
(c) That some form of distraction or concurrent ritual during exposure—any believable addition—may maximize therapeutic or placebo response—which is interesting, but is not advanced by claims that Arbitrary Ritual X is the magic one that cures all problems.

In summary, regarding Feinstein's (2014a) three assertions:

(a) There is still no substantial evidence supporting the efficacy of those elements that are unique and essential to energy psychology. Feinstein has argued that the shallow, muddy swamp of poorly controlled supportive studies is "accumulating," but a broader swamp provides no greater clarity. The only two attempts to dive deeper (Pignotti, 2005; Waite & Holder, 2003) have produced *dis*confirmatory results, and have been ignored by Feinstein on shifting, and what therefore seem post hoc, criteria. His data remain skewed, and support has "flat-lined."
(b) The claim that energy psychology techniques are "surprisingly rapid and effective" should make them more easily confirmed in properly controlled studies. When they are not, the rapidity of powerful placebo responses is implied.
(c) The evidence in support of the existence of meridians, thought fields, subtle and mysterious energy fields, and even the efficacy of acupuncture, remains negligible. This makes the claims of energy psychology all the more extraordinary, the required supportive evidence all the more substantial and extraordinary, and the current state of evidence even more "less than ordinary." The only "plausible

mechanisms [that] are consistent with established psychological principles," such as placebo, expectancy, relationship factors, imaginal exposure, or other concurrent cognitive behavior therapy processes, are not new and are not part of "energy psychology."

References

Bakker, G. M. (2013). The current status of energy psychology: Extraordinary claims with less than ordinary evidence. *Clinical Psychologist, 17*(3), 91–99. doi:101111/cp.12020

Benedetti, F. (2009). *Placebo effects: Understanding the mechanisms in health and disease*. Oxford: Oxford University Press.

Callahan, R. (1985). *Five minute phobia cure*. Wilmington, DE: Enterprise.

David, D., & Montgomery, G. H. (2011). The scientific status of psychotherapies. *Clinical Psychology: Science and Practice, 18*(2), 89–99.

Eisner, D. A. (2000). *The death of psychotherapy: From Freud to alien abductions*. Westport, CT: Praeger.

Feinstein, D. (2008). Energy psychology: A review of the preliminary evidence. *Psychotherapy: Theory, Research, Practice, Training, 45*(2), 199–213. doi:10.1037/0033-3204.45.2.199.

Feinstein, D. (2009). Facts, paradigms, and anomalies in the acceptance of energy psychology: A rejoinder to McCaslin's (2009) and Pignotti and Thyer's (2009) comments on Feinstein (2008a). *Psychotherapy: Theory, Research, Practice, Training, 46*(2), 262–269. doi:10.1037/a0016086.

Feinstein, D. (2012). Acupoint stimulation in treating psychological disorders: Evidence of efficacy. *Review of General Psychology, 16*(4), 364–380. doi:10.1037/a0028602.

Feinstein, D. (2013). Energy psychology treatments over a distance: The curious phenomenon of "surrogate tapping." *Energy Psychology: Theory, Research, and Treatment, 5*(1), 32–43. doi:10.9769.EPJ.2013.5.1.DF

Feinstein D. (2014a). Comment on 'The current status of energy psychology': Growing evidence for extraordinary claims. *Energy Psychology: Theory, Research, and Treatment, 6*(1).

Feinstein, D. (2014b). Endorsement quotation on homepage of https://www.havening.org retrieved January 11, 2014.

Feinstein, D., & Church, D. (2010). Modulating gene expression through psychotherapy: The contribution of noninvasive somatic interventions. *Review of General Psychology, 14*(4), 283–295. doi:10.1037/a0021252.

Gaudiano, B. A., Brown, L. A., & Miller, I. W. (2012). Tapping their patients' problems away? Characteristics of psychotherapists using energy meridian techniques. *Research on Social Work Practice, 22*, 647–655.

Herbert, J. D., & Gaudiano, B. A. (2005). Moving from empirically supported treatment lists to practice guidelines in psychotherapy: The role of the placebo concept. *Journal of Clinical Psychology, 61*(7), 893–908. doi:10.1002/jclp.20133.

Langevin, H. M., & Yandow, J. A. (2002). Relationship of acupuncture points and meridians to connective tissue planes. *Anatomical Record, 269*, 257–265. doi:10.1002/ar.10185.

Lilienfeld, S. O. (1998). Pseudoscience in contemporary clinical psychology: What it is and what we can do about it. *Clinical Psychologist, 51*(4), 3–9.

Lilienfeld, S. O., Lynn, S. J., & Lohr, J. M. (Eds.) (2003). *Science and pseudoscience in clinical psychology*. New York: Guilford Press.

Pignotti, M. (2005). Thought Field Therapy Voice Technology vs. random meridian point sequences: A single-blind controlled experiment. *Scientific Review of Mental Health Practice, 4*(1), 38–47.

Rosen, G. M., & Davison, G. C. (2003). Psychology should list empirically supported principles of change (ESPs) and not credential trademarked therapies or other treatment packages. *Behavior Modification, 27*(3), 300–312. doi:10.1177/0145445503027003003.

Ruden, S. J., & Ruden, R. A. (2010). Treating the phobic and anxious dental patient: Introduction to Havening Therapy. *Dentistrytoday.com*, April.

Waite, W. L., & Holder, M. D. (2003). Assessment of the Emotional Freedom Technique: An alternative treatment for fear. *Scientific Review of Mental Health Practice, 2*, 20–26.

REVIEW ARTICLE

Calling an Avalanche a Swamp: Comments on Bakker (2014)

David Feinstein

Correspondence: David Feinstein, PhD, 777 East Main Street, Ashland, OR 97520. Tel: 541-482-1800; Fax: 772-382-8555; Email: df777@earthlink.net

Gary Bakker maintains, in "A Bigger Swamp Is Still a Swamp" (2014), that "support for energy psychology's efficacy has flat-lined" (p. 44) and that the rapid outcomes claimed by the method's proponents can be reasonably explained as the effects of exposure, placebo, expectancy, the therapeutic relationship, or other influences that are extraneous to the method's distinctive procedures. This reply will attempt to establish that neither is the case, and it will address additional issues raised by Bakker.

Is Evidence for Tapping Flat-lining or Mounting?

Three-fourths of the 51 studies or outcome reports appearing in peer-reviewed journals that met the inclusion criteria of my most recent review article (Feinstein, 2012) were published in the 4 years since my initial exploratory review (Feinstein, 2008). This did not suggest that the emerging support for energy psychology's efficacy was trending toward becoming "flat-lined." A review of EFT studies published 9 months later (Church, 2013) cites 14 additional investigations, including five randomized controlled trials (RCTs), that appeared after my 2012 review. Among the conditions examined were PTSD, traumatic brain injury, anxiety, depression, addiction, pain reduction, insomnia, weight loss, test-taking, and sports performance. These investigations have appeared at a slightly faster pace than in the 4 years between my first and second reviews, and they were consistent with my finding that the vast preponderance of studies reported strong positive outcomes. Again, this hardly qualifies as having "flat-lined." In addition, as the methodological rigor of the studies has increased markedly from my 2008 to my 2012 reviews, the professed swamp analogy grows even less tenable. In fact, as professional and popular interest in energy psychology is accelerating (the top five EFT websites had more than six million visitors in the month of June 2013, according to an analysis done on http://www.trafficestimate.com), the more apt comparison might be to an avalanche than to a swamp.

Is Tapping an "Active Ingredient" in the Reported Positive Outcomes of Energy Psychology Treatments?

This is one of Bakker's most pivotal questions. Whether tapping on acupuncture points is an active ingredient, an inert placebo, or simply a distraction was addressed directly in a dismantling study by Fox (2013). Twenty college students received one of two treatment protocols targeting emotions related to academic achievement. One group received an EFT treatment as described in *The EFT Manual* (Craig, 2011); the other received the same protocol, including all the exposure elements of EFT, but without tapping on acupuncture points. Instead, they utilized a mindfulness procedure along with focused breathing wherever tapping was called for in the EFT protocol. On a standardized self-report of achievement-related emotions, the tapping participants experienced a greater increase of "positive emotions" such as enjoyment, hope, and pride ($p < .01$) and a greater decrease of "negative emotions" such as anger, hopelessness, and shame ($p < .01$). While the study's weaknesses included the small sample size, lack of long-term follow-up, and the possibility of experimenter bias, it provided reasonable basis to conclude that the tapping was a potent active ingredient.

Fox's conclusions are consistent with the findings of an earlier RCT in which two comparison conditions utilized the cognitive and exposure elements of EFT while one used tapping and the other substituted tapping with diaphragmatic breathing in treating fears of small animals

(Wells, Polglase, Andrews, Carrington, & Baker, 2003). Participants in both groups improved, but the improvement was significantly greater for the tapping group in four of five assessment areas (all but pulse rate), including a measurable fear-based behavior in an in-vivo situation ($p < .02$), self-reported fear in an in-vivo situation ($p < .02$), self-reported fear in an imagined situation ($p < .005$), and a standardized fear questionnaire ($p < .005$). Bakker (2013) minimized these findings as showing that "EFT slightly outperformed diaphragmatic breathing" (p. 94) and, despite Wells et al. reporting that the significant differences between the two groups held on follow-up for several (but not all) measures, Bakker gives the impression that the differences between the groups "decreased on follow-up" (p. 94) for all the measures. After a detailed analysis of the studies comprising my 2012 review, I was able to conclude, to the satisfaction of the editor and reviewers of the journal of the American Psychological Association's Division 1, that studies meeting "accepted scientific standards" in investigating the use of acupoint stimulation for treating psychological disorders have "consistently demonstrated strong effect sizes and other positive statistical results that far exceed chance after relatively few treatment sessions" (Feinstein, 2012, p. 377).

Is a Consensus in Sight?

Some of Bakker's criticisms of the existing research are, nonetheless, apt. While Thought Field Therapy, the initial energy psychology protocol, has been around since the 1980s, serious research is very recent and is, in the absence of government and university support, most often conducted with no outside funding. In my 2012 paper, I clearly acknowledged that future clinical trials need to be conducted by "disinterested investigators utilizing the rigorously designed studies that can be expected as the broader psychological community scrutinizes energy psychology interventions" (Feinstein, 2012, p. 375).

Bakker and I agree on this basic point: More stringent research supporting the efficacy of energy psychology protocols needs to be produced before definitive conclusions about its effectiveness can be rendered. Still, some two dozen supportive RCTs can be found in the literature. That Bakker (and other commentators such as Gaudiano, Brown, & Miller, 2012; McCaslin, 2009; Pignotti & Thyer, 2009) can, based on the same data, come to such divergent conclusions from the thousands of psychotherapists who practice energy psychology is interesting in itself.

Do the Differing Conclusions Trace to a Clash of Paradigms?

One interpretation has been that the controversies stem in part from a paradigmatic clash within the professional community. Energy psychology has become a lightning rod because its explanatory accounts include "subtle energies" that are derived from the health and mental health traditions of other cultures (Feinstein, 2009), often unfamiliar or quite foreign to a Western mind that says, "If we can't measure it, it's not real." This resistance is further exacerbated by energy psychology's odd-looking procedures and claims of outcomes that are more rapid than can be reconciled with the clinical experiences of most therapists.

Even the studies by Pignotti (2005) and Waite and Holder (2003) that Bakker criticizes me for discounting showed tapping to be followed by significant improvements based on extremely brief, single-session treatments. Pignotti reported that after a telephone tapping session, "97% of the 66 participants reported a complete elimination of all subjective emotional distress" (Pignotti, 2005, p. 38). Waite and Holder found that three groups that used tapping under different conditions (even if one involved tapping one's index finger on a doll) all showed significant reductions in self-reported fear ($p < .003$, .001, and .001) while a non-tapping group did not. It is interesting that adversarial camps (e.g., Bakker, 2014; Feinstein, 2009) both point to these highly flawed studies (e.g., Pasahow, 2010) as supporting their positions. Bakker and other critics of energy psychology who have examined this research have ignored how dramatic the improvements appear to have been, proclaiming that any gains were caused by factors unrelated to the tapping. Proponents of the method note: a) both of Waite and Holder's tapping control conditions may have inadvertently been stimulating acupuncture points—even the seemingly farcical "doll" condition stimulates an acupuncture point (Large Intestine 1) that is used by acupuncturists in the treatment of "mental restlessness" (Ross, 1995, p. 306), and b) that while Pignotti demonstrated that the order and selection from 10 TFT tapping points is not important despite the claims of the method's founder, she also demonstrated that tapping even a random selection of TFT points in any order resulted consistently in strong decreases of reported emotional distress.

Clinicians who employ energy psychology are also familiar with reports of its rapid positive outcomes leading to cognitive dissonance—or outright dismissal—in conventionally trained clinicians. As Thomas Kuhn (1996) emphasized, in the 50th anniversary edition of his classic work on the way scientific thought progresses, when "confronted by even severe and prolonged anomalies, [scientists] do not renounce the paradigm" (p. 77). Energy psychology is at the center of a perfect storm bred of cognitive dissonance and paradigm clashes. When a client with a lifelong fear of snakes taps on a series of points on the skin while making statements related to the fear can, after 20 minutes, calmly hold a lab technician's pet boa, we have an outcome that cannot readily be explained by conventional clinical paradigms but that can easily be dismissed as a mere anomaly. When thousands of parallel case reports have been entered into the public record (e.g., www.EFTUniverse.com), coming from practitioners whose allegiances are far removed from the method's founders or even their direct protégés, we have a series of "severe and prolonged" anomalies. When the explanations that are rendered trace to ancient healing and spiritual traditions rather than scientific findings, the paradigm clash deepens.

When conventional paradigms are challenged, sardonic characterizations of innovations emerging from outside the mainstream are not unusual, such as Bakker's depiction of Havening therapy (2014, p. 44). Havening was developed by Ron Ruden, an internist who had previously established himself as among the leading authorities on how advances in the neurosciences can support the treatment of disorders such as addictions and obesity (Ruden, 2000). Having pioneered computer models of chemical synthesis with Nobel laureate E. J. Corey at Harvard, Ruden was surprised to find that such a seemingly benign intervention as tapping on the body could lead to rapid positive outcomes in trauma treatment, and he formulated a neurological explanation of the mechanisms involved (Ruden, 2010). I have described Ruden's theoretical formulation as a "monumental accomplishment" and was surprised to be quoted out of context as having used the term as a blanket endorsement of the method (Bakker, 2014, p. 44) when the comment was focusing on the theoretical contribution.

Does Raising the Bar for More Stringent Research Necessarily Resolve Paradigm Clashes?

Clinical innovation begins when a therapist—based on instinct, chance, or theoretical calculation—does something atypical with a client and it appears to have a beneficial effect. The novel operation is then repeated or applied with additional clients. If successes are observed, informal or formal reports about these early outcomes bring the method to the attention of other clinicians. Behavioral therapy and cognitive therapy, for instance, were first introduced in books presenting multiple case histories, not in peer-reviewed papers providing evidence from controlled studies (Mollon, 2007). Eventually, however, there is enough reason to believe that the approach merits systematic investigation. This might begin with standardized pre- and post-treatment assessments. If these findings are encouraging, the investigation is typically extended to larger numbers. Next, the more stringent requirements of RCTs, such as well-defined control conditions and randomization, are introduced. For some, this progression, if consistently showing positive outcomes, is an adequate demonstration that the approach has merit. But the bar can be raised ever higher.

The ways of controlling for extraneous variables are, in fact, almost endless. Among the possible considerations for an RCT, beyond proper randomization and comparison conditions, are large sample sizes, sophisticated methods for defining treatment populations, use of structured diagnostic interviews or other measures that are more objective than self-reports, assessment tools that meet the most rigorous requirements of validity and reliability, assurance that treatment manuals have been strictly adhered to by those administering the therapy, application of ever more exacting statistical methods, scrutinizing the components of a treatment to assess their active and inactive ingredients and possible interactive effects, and controlling for any bias or allegiances of those doing the treatment or interpreting the data, etc.

These escalating requirements almost ensure that the only settings for research that meet the highest standards are likely to be well-funded, established institutions—the very voices of conventional paradigms and prevailing economic interests. The scientific rationale for this trade-off is that it controls for extraneous variables. However, a point of diminishing returns is eventually reached wherein increasingly stringent research standards do not significantly increase the confidence with which a study's findings can be interpreted. In fact, one of the fallacies in the thinking of those who adhere to exorbitant criteria in evaluating clinical innovation (the "pseudoskeptics") is to assume that the *possibility* of extraneous influences in an experiment *explains* unexpected findings (that is, findings that don't conform to the prevailing paradigm) so those findings can be discounted (Feinstein, 2009).

Have Wait-list Research Designs Provided Any Valid Clinical Information?

This is not to argue for shoddy research. One of Bakker's most adamant criticisms of the RCTs that support the efficacy of energy psychology is that many of them utilize wait-list instead of alternative-treatment comparison conditions. Wait-list control designs are widely accepted in establishing the efficacy of psychological treatments (Chambless & Hollon, 1998). They are also regularly admitted in investigating the evidence-based status of cognitive, exposure, and other therapies on the "Website on Research-Supported Psychological Treatments" maintained by Division 12 of the American Psychological Association (http://www.div12.org/PsychologicalTreatments/index.html). Nonetheless, wait-list designs "do not control for placebo, suggestion, or expectation" (Feinstein, 2012, p. 374). Therefore, can it be ruled out that the strong, positive outcomes reported in the vast majority of energy psychology RCTs that use wait-lists as their only control are not based on such extraneous factors?

Nine of the 18 RCTs in my review (Feinstein, 2012) included an alternative-treatment control condition while the other nine used only a wait-list control. Statistical significance in the outcomes were "roughly equivalent for the studies that used only a wait-list (*p* levels for their strongest major findings were .05, .001, .001, .001, .001, .001, .001, .001, and .001 respectively)" in comparison to "studies that used a placebo or active ingredient treatment (*p* levels for their strongest major finding were .05, .05, .05, .03, .005, .001, .001, and .001 respectively, with one study not providing a *p* score in establishing significance)" (p. 374). Active ingredient controls, or even controls that use active interventions with no known therapeutic agents, tend to equalize suggestion, expectancy, and other extraneous factors. Not only did the energy psychology treatments far exceed the effects of the wait-list conditions in all of the wait-list control studies, they also significantly exceeded the effects of active ingredient controls in most of the studies using an active ingredient comparison condition.

In terms of the choice of a comparison condition, an analysis of psychotherapy research designs concluded that a supportive clinical interview is the best available active control condition for nonspecific effects such as sympathetic attention and expectancy (Behar & Borkovec, 2003). Two RCTs (Baker & Siegel, 2010; Church, Yount, & Brooks, 2012) showed energy psychology treatments to produce significantly stronger outcomes than supportive interviews. In addition, findings such as 86% of veterans going from above to below PTSD cutoffs after six EFT treatment sessions (Church et al., 2013) are not only unmatched by studies of other treatments, there is no evidence suggesting that placebo or other nonspecific ingredients can produce comparable improvements with PTSD.

Has a Reasonable Research Threshold Been Met?

Given the multiple sets of standards that can be applied when evaluating clinical trials, psychotherapists reviewing available evidence have a choice about where to draw the line regarding what constitutes reasonable grounds for deciding to incorporate a new therapy into their practices. In the case of energy psychology, efficacy research has progressed in a dozen years from no peer-reviewed investigations to two dozen RCTs with increasingly strong designs. Both the APA's Division 12 (Chambless & Hollon, 1998) and the U.S. Food and Drug Administration (1998) require only two independent RCTs to establish that a treatment has demonstrated effectiveness for a specified condition, a threshold that is based on sound rationale (both scientific and practical—for instance, it does not advance the frontiers of science to have the same experiment repeated again and again). As research provides mounting evidence for the efficacy of energy psychology while its critics continue to portray that evidence as being inadequate (e.g., Bakker, 2013, 2014; Gaudiano et al., 2012), the onus shifts to the critics to provide a uniform set of standards that can be applied to any psychotherapy in establishing efficacy if the Division 12 standards or other recognized standards are not adequate.

Is Energy Psychology in Widespread Use?

The context surrounding scientific investigation is also relevant in making such important, practical decisions. Clinical experience, for instance, appropriately informs research findings. While many established institutions—such as the military, the Veterans Administration, and many hospitals—still do not recognize energy psychology as an evidence-based treatment, thousands of clinicians have reported that the method is rapid and potent (see, for instance, the more than 5,000 case histories posted on www.EFTUniverse.com).

Bakker (2014) claims that my citation of the survey by Gaudiano et al. (2012) "misrepresents the growth in popularity of energy psychology among therapists" (p. 44). But even if the finding by Gaudiano et al. (2012) that 42.3% of the 149 therapists responding to their survey said they "frequently use or are inclined to use" energy meridian techniques (p. 647) is based on a skewed sampling, energy psychology is increasingly being practiced in clinical settings as well as on a self-help basis. Gaudiano et al. (2012) speculated that the high percentage they found—in comparison to two earlier surveys that showed 9% and 19%, respectively—is possibly "explained by the increasing popularity of these methods" (p. 650). At the time of this writing, more than half a million people had participated in each of the last four annual online World Tapping Summits and over two million people had downloaded a manual that gives instructions for using energy psychology on a self-help basis. These are, in all likelihood, unprecedented numbers for any psychological self-help approach. While popular appeal is not an arbiter of scientific validity, the word-of-mouth and electronic media testimonials that have resulted in these numbers correspond with the research that has so far been produced.

Why Is Energy Psychology Not More Widely Recognized by the Profession If the General Public and Growing Numbers of Clinicians Are Finding it Effective?

If energy psychology is effective, why is it not more widely recognized within the psychotherapy establishment? A monograph by the Institute of Medicine of the National Academy of Science—*Crossing the Quality Chasm: A New Health System for the 21st Century*—reported that "an average of about 17 years is required for new knowledge generated by randomized controlled trials to be incorporated into practice" (Committee on Quality of Health Care in America, Institute of Medicine, 2001, p. 13). Lamenting the "insufficient tools and incentives to promote rapid adoption of best practices," the report notes that "current dissemination efforts fail to reach many clinicians and patients" (p. 14). Perhaps energy psychology is on course. A decade ago, almost no empirical research supporting the efficacy of energy psychology existed, although the 17-year translational gap may be further extended by the fact that elements of the approach do not conform to established clinical paradigms. On the other hand, the surveys showing that between 9% and 43% of therapists use or are inclined to use energy therapies, along with the American Psychological Association's recent decision to recognize training in energy psychology as a legitimate topic for APA-approved continuing education, suggest that the translational gap may already be narrowing.

Are Meridians—a Core Concept in Explanations of the Mechanisms of Action in Energy Psychology—Real?

Also helping close this gap are findings in related fields establishing physiological structures that correspond with traditional maps of acupuncture points and meridians. Bakker (2014) cites an anatomical study by Langevin and Yandow (2002) and correctly notes that their findings showed "an 80% correspondence between acupuncture points and the location of connective tissue planes in post-mortem tissue sections" (2014, p. 44), but he incorrectly asserts that they "did not find meridians. No one has." (p. 44). Langevin and Yandow actually found that three of the six meridians they examined, as shown in traditional charts, "coincide with intermuscular or intramuscular connective tissue planes" (p. 263). The earliest physiological study to claim to have identified meridian pathways was conducted in North Korea (Kim, 1963) and involved injecting acupuncture points with dyes and observing that the dye followed predicted meridian pathways. In part because the exact methods were not described in the research report, it was not replicated for over 50 years, lending doubt to its veracity. Finally, in 2002, a team at Seoul National University began to replicate the studies and has been able to verify many of the original findings (Soh, Kang, & Ryu, 2013).

Meanwhile, CT (computerized tomography) scans have revealed the anatomical structure of acupuncture points (Chenglin et al., in press), acupuncture points have been found to have distinct electrical properties (Ahn et al., 2008), and a recent systematic review of 29 RCTs of acupuncture in the treatment of chronic pain, involving almost 18,000 patients, concluded both that acupuncture is effective and that it is more than just a placebo (Vickers et al., 2012). Directly pertinent to treating psychological conditions, fMRI (functional magnetic resonance imaging) studies conducted at Harvard Medical School have demonstrated that the stimulation of selected acupuncture points sends deactivating signals to the amygdala and other areas of the limbic system (Fang et al., 2009).

Conclusion

The dialectic between the thoughtful proponent and the sincere skeptic, as witnessed in this series of exchanges, may not necessarily persuade either party, but it highlights issues the field must address. On the one side, within our professional responsibilities to the public, we should adhere to the highest reasonable research standards before conferring evidence-based status to another new therapy. On the other side, when enough sources of information indicate that an innovation offers potent benefits to those suffering with serious psychological disorders, public welfare is served when the translational gap is closed and such best practices are adopted.

References

Ahn, A. C., Colbert, A. P., Anderson, B. J., Martinsen, O. G., Hammerschlag, R., Cina, S., ... Langevin, H. M. (2008). Electrical properties of acupuncture points and meridians: A systematic review. *Bioelectromagnetics*, *29*, 245–256. doi:10.1002/bem.20403

Baker, A. H., & Siegel, M. A. (2010). Emotional Freedom Techniques (EFT) reduces intense fears: A partial replication and extension of Wells et al. *Energy Psychology: Theory, Research, and Treatment*, *2*(2), 13–30.

Bakker, G. M. (2013, November). The current status of energy psychology: Extraordinary claims with less than ordinary evidence. *Clinical Psychologist*, *17*(3), 91–99. Article first published online, July 30, 2013. doi:10.1111/cp.12020

Bakker, G. M. (2014). A bigger swamp is still a swamp: Comments on Feinstein (2014). *Energy Psychology: Theory, Research, and Treatment*, *6*(1), 44–47.

Behar, E. S., & Borkovec, T. D. (2003). Psychotherapy outcome research. In I. B. Weiner, *Handbook of Psychology* (2nd ed., Vol. 2: *Research Methods in Psychology*, pp. 213–240). New York, NY: Wiley. doi:10.1002/9781118133880

Chambless, D. L, & Hollon, S. D. (1998). Defining empirically supported therapies. *Journal of Consulting and Clinical Psychology*, *66*, 7–18. doi:10.1037/0022-006X.66.1.7

Chenglin, L., Xiaohua, W., Hua, X., Fank, L., Ruishan, D., Dongming, Z., ... Tiqiao, X. (In press). X-ray phase-contrast CT imaging of the acupoints based on synchrotron radiation. *Journal of Electron Spectroscopy and Related Phenomena.* Retrieved from http://dx.doi.org/10.1016/j.elspec.2013.12.005

Church, D. (2013). Clinical EFT as an evidence-based practice for the treatment of psychological and physiological conditions. *Psychology*, *4*, 645–654. doi:10.4236/psych.2013.48092

Church, D., Hawk, C., Brooks, A., Toukolehto, O., Wren, M., Dinter, I., & Stein, P. (2013). Psychological trauma in veterans using EFT (Emotional Freedom Techniques): A randomized controlled trial. *Journal of Nervous and Mental Disease*, *201*, 153–160. doi:10.1097/NMD.0b013e31827f6351

Church, D., Yount, G., & Brooks, A. (2012). The effect of Emotional Freedom Techniques (EFT) on stress biochemistry: A randomized controlled trial. *Journal of Nervous and Mental Disease*, *200*, 891–896. doi:10.1097/NMD.0b013e31826b9fc1

Committee on Quality of Health Care in America, Institute of Medicine. (2001). *Crossing the quality chasm: A new health system for the 21st century.* Washington, DC: National Academy Press.

Craig, G. (2011). *The EFT manual* (2nd ed.). Santa Rosa, CA: Energy Psychology Press.

Fang, J., Jin, Z., Wang, Y., Li, K., Kong, J., Nixon, E. E., ... Hui, K. K.-S. (2009). The salient characteristics of the central effects of acupuncture needling: Limbic-paralimbic-neocortical network modulation. *Human Brain Mapping*, *30*, 1196–1206. doi:10.1002/hbm.20583

Feinstein, D. (2008). Energy psychology: A review of the preliminary evidence. *Psychotherapy: Theory, Research, Practice, Training*, *45*(2), 199–213. doi:10.1037/0033-3204.45.2.199

Feinstein, D. (2009). Facts, paradigms, and anomalies in the acceptance of energy psychology: A rejoinder to McCaslin's (2009) and Pignotti and Thyer's (2009) comments on Feinstein (2008a). *Psychotherapy: Theory, Research, Practice, Training*, *46*(2), 262–269. doi:10.1037/a0016086

Feinstein, D. (2012). Acupoint stimulation in treating psychological disorders: Evidence of efficacy. *Review of General Psychology*, *16*(4), 364–380. doi:10.1037/a0028602

Food and Drug Administration. (1998). *Guidance for industry: Providing clinical evidence of effectiveness for human drug and biological products.* Rockville, MD: U.S. Department of Health and Human Services.

Fox, L. (2013). Is acupoint tapping an active ingredient or an inert placebo in Emotional Freedom Techniques (EFT)? A randomized controlled dismantling study. *Energy Psychology: Theory, Research, and Treatment*, *5*(2), 15–28.

Gaudiano, B. A., Brown, L. A., & Miller, I. W. (2012). Tapping their patients' problems away? Characteristics of psychotherapists using energy meridian techniques. *Research on Social Work Practice*, *22*, 647–655. doi:10.1177/1049731512448468

Kim, B. H. (1963). On the acupuncture meridian system. *Journal of Jo Sun Medicine*, *90*, 6–35.

Kuhn, T. S. (1996). *The structure of scientific revolutions* (3rd ed.). Chicago, IL: University of Chicago Press.

Langevin, H. M., & Yandow, J. A. (2002). Relationship of acupuncture points and meridians to connective tissue planes. *Anatomical Record*, *269*, 257–265. doi:10.1002/ar.10185

McCaslin, D. (2009). A review of efficacy claims in energy psychology. *Psychotherapy: Research, Practice, Training*, *46*, 249–256. doi:10.1037/a0016025

Mollon, P. (2007). Debunking the pseudoscience debunkers. *Clinical Psychology Forum* (a monthly publication of the British Psychological Society's Division of Clinical Psychology), Issue *174*, 13–16.

Pasahow, R. (2010). Methodological problems in Waite and Holder (2003) preclude meaningful interpretations about Emotional Freedom Techniques (EFT). *Energy Psychology: Theory, Research, and Treatment*, *2*(2), 57–72. doi:10.9769.EPJ.2010.2.2.RP

Pignotti, M. (2005). Thought Field Therapy Voice Technology vs. random meridian point sequences: A single-blind controlled experiment. *Scientific Review of Mental Health Practice*, *4*(1), 72–81.

Pignotti, M., & Thyer, B. (2009). Some comments on "Energy Psychology: A Review of the Evidence": Premature conclusions based on incomplete evidence? *Psychotherapy: Research, Practice, Training*, *46*, 257–261. doi:10.1037/a0016027

Ross, J. (1995). *Acupuncture point combinations: The key to clinical success*. Philadelphia, PA: Churchill Livingstone.

Ruden, R. A. (2000). *The craving brain*. New York, NY: Harper Perennial.

Ruden, R. A. (2010). *When the past is always present: Emotional traumatization, causes, and cures*. New York, NY: Routledge.

Soh, K-S., Kang, K. A., & Ryu, Y. H. (2013). 50 years of Bong-Han theory and 10 years of primo vascular system. *Evidence-Based Complementary and Alternative Medicine, 2013*, Article ID 587827. doi:10.1155/2013/587827

Vickers, A. J., Cronin, A. M., Maschino, A. C., Lewith, G., MacPherson, H., Foster, N. E., … Linde, K. (2012). Acupuncture for chronic pain: Individual patient data meta-analysis. *Archives of Internal Medicine*, *172,* 1444–1453. doi:10.1001/archinternmed.2012.3654

Waite, L. W., & Holder, M. D. (2003). Assessment of the emotional freedom technique: An alternative treatment for fear. *Scientific Review of Mental Health Practice*, *2*(1), 20–26.

Wells, S., Polglase, K., Andrews, H. B., Carrington, P., & Baker, A. H. (2003). Evaluation of a meridian-based intervention, emotional freedom techniques (EFT), for reducing specific phobias of small animals. *Journal of Clinical Psychology*, *59*, 943–966. doi:10.1002/jclp.10189

Heal Yourself with Emotional Freedom Technique: A Teach Yourself Guide

John Freedom

McGraw-Hill, 2013
Softcover, 256 pages
$16.00
ISBN 978-1-4441-7718-3

Reviewed by Cary Bell

In *Heal Yourself with Emotional Freedom Technique*, author John Freedom teaches EFT by breaking down a complex subject into digestible chapters, while at the same time presenting background, stories, and case studies that engage the reader.

Freedom, an EFT practitioner and educator, suggests that the book can be read in different ways: "This is your book! Adapt it and make it your own." Chapters 1–4 cover the what and the why of EFT; chapter 5 is when the tapping lessons begin.

I personally liked reading the book in order, and then going back and rereading, or doing exercises from, certain chapters. This is easily done thanks to summary points throughout the chapter and at the end of the chapter. The summary points serve as a highlighter and are helpful to come back to as a chapter refresher. The reader can jump to specific spots in the book and reference specific topics easily.

Before Freedom teaches the basic formula of EFT, he provides the reader with background on energy medicine and the healing power of touch. This is especially good for those readers who may be on the fence about the subject and those who want to grasp the concept fully. Here, Freedom introduces the basic premise of the book: What you feel, you can heal.

An entire chapter is devoted to breaking through blocks and walls. He compares physically tapping to tapping on a rusty pipe; both release patterns of obstruction, or blocks. From there, the reader understands the why of tapping, and the next chapter teaches how to tap.

The how-to chapter gives a step-by-step description of how to practice EFT. The guide is easy to understand and use. If you've practiced EFT before, it serves as a refresher, with tips and suggestions that may be new to you.

Freedom says the basic recipe constitutes about 20% of the healing treasure chest; to get the most out of EFT requires going deeper. He walks the reader through ways to go deeper and fine-tune results. The remainder of the book goes into tapping for specific issues.

Each chapter includes examples of EFT and practice exercises to help guide the reader through the process. Case studies are also included to show different ways tapping is used, as well as to motivate readers by showing them the possibilities of EFT.

Freedom has an easy-to-read style that simplifies a complex subject. Anyone from a novice to an expert would benefit from, and enjoy, *Heal Yourself with Emotional Freedom Technique*.

Epiphany: True Stories of Sudden Insight to Inspire, Encourage, and Transform

Elise Ballard
Harmony Books, 2011
Hardcover, 299 pages
$22.99
ISBN 978-0-307-71610-1

Reviewed by Lucie Monroe, EFT INT-1

When actress, film-maker, and producer Elise Ballard experienced what she describes as a defining moment during which she both faced one of her deepest fears and gained freedom from it, she didn't know it was going to change her and teach her an important life lesson. She realized in retrospect that what she had experienced was an epiphany, defined as a moment of great or sudden revelation; an intuitive grasp of reality through something usually simple and striking; an illuminating discovery, realization, or disclosure. She became fascinated with the power that this life-changing moment held for her. She started asking her friends, family, and acquaintances about their own major, life-altering breakthroughs, revelations, realizations, awakenings, or "aha" moments and how they impacted their lives. After discovering that most people didn't talk about their defining moments, her interest grew and she started conducting interviews on a larger scale and putting them up on her website (www.epiphanychannel.com). In this book, she discusses the nature and the power of epiphanies, and offers 59 stories of personal epiphany from acquaintances and public figures alike. The stories are divided into the six different categories: awakenings, new directions, healings, miracles, comings of age, and callings. They also always involve the four following elements: listening, belief, action, and serendipity. This book weaves poignant stories in an inspiring narrative, illustrating beautifully the power of thoughts and how one meaningful cognitive shift can change one's outlook and influence one's destiny.

The Practical Visionary: A New World Guide to Spiritual Growth and Social Change

Corinne McLaughlin with Gordon Davidson
Unity House, 2010
Softcover, 316 pages
$18.17
ISBN 978-0-8715-9340-5

Reviewed by Charles C. Crenshaw Jr.

By the author of *Builders of the Dawn: Community Lifestyle in a Changing World*, a classic from the 1990s, *The Practical Visionary* brings the practical application of what Corinne McLaughlin has learned to a present-day audience. *Builders of the Dawn* dealt with the author's experience in intentional communities. The knowledge she gleaned there helped her develop a philosophy that is quite meaningful for today's world. She saw firsthand how building community aided individuals in getting more involved with the environment and the evolution of our human species.

Not all OM and Namastes, however, McLaughlin lets the reader in on little-known facts about meditation in the world scene. She tells us that the practice of meditation has even reached places like the Pentagon. Yes, the Pentagon has had a meditation room for the last 30 years, the last place you would expect there to be one. Of all things, McLaughlin taught meditation classes there.

The Practical Visionary explains how the benefits of meditation, and the worldview related to it, are more than just the musings of some cloistered mystic. In each chapter of what the author calls a New World guide, she provides one of eight keys to spiritual growth and social change. She does this with a view to help us shift from what is dying or becoming passé in our local and world culture, to what is rising, or will rise, from those ashes like a phoenix. She suggests that if we understand the evolutionary plan and look at the big picture behind our recent financial crises and other world events, we can become peaceful cocreators in the evolutionary process. The author suggests that what has happened recently does not have to be viewed as gloom and doom. It is all about how things must change in order for us to progress. She argues that if we make our livelihood a social change strategy, involving what she calls "the magic of our souls," looking inside ourselves for a source of spiritual strength, and viewing money as a spiritual asset versus a means for self-aggrandizement, then we can transform our global conflicts. Our conflicts can become a means for working toward a higher synthesis instead of a means for building walls between us. The meditations the author presents at the end of each chapter are there to help us overcome the blocks that might be hindering our envisioning a peaceful and sustainable world. A noble endeavor indeed, *The Practical Visionary* is a book rightly named, being both practical and visionary.

This Will Change Everything: Ideas that Will Shape the Future

Edited by John Brockman

Harper Perennial, 2009
Softcover, 390 pages
$14.99
ISBN 978-0-0618-9967-6

Reviewed by David Pierotti

Every year Edge.org asks an "annual question" to be answered by the brightest and most forward thinking of our time. Brockman and company's vision is to "arrive at the edge of the world's knowledge, seek out the most complex and sophisticated minds, put them in a room together, and have them ask each other the questions they are asking themselves." I would argue that they have succeeded in that mission with *This Will Change Everything*, but only just.

The topics explored are many and varied, ranging from commentary on advanced genetic engineering, climate, food supply, human consciousness merging with robotics, artificial intelligence, and quantum computers to alien life, neuroscience, free energy, and more. Among the 125 contributors' mini-essays, all readers will find topics that will resonate with how they see the world—there is something for everyone here.

Authors speak of exciting visionary innovations that would shift the global lifestyle in myriad incogitable directions. Yet other writers talk of collapse of societies and planet Earth at the hand of our cumulative mistakes in energy, economics, population growth, and nuclear weaponry. There is a healthy balance of that lively optimistic forethought mixed with a necessary forecast of what could happen if our actions as a group of seven billion are not kept in check.

The abounding majority of authors write succinct, thought-provoking, and paradigm-shifting commentary; however, there a few that slip through the cracks. These straggling few still talk of time-tested and failed beliefs that are cradled closely probably because of their professional credentials and allegiance that will not allow the next direction in that field to occur.

What is interesting is the lack of any essays on a government or policy that will have the ability to change everything. Petty bickering and one-upmanship lead to more of the same, devoid of any real progress. It is only through science, philosophy, business, and various practical arts that paradigm-altering ideas manifest to the world en masse.

Many of the authors write from a belief of dogmatic materialism, living in a world where the human mind is a tangible thing made up of biological squishy stuff, the chemical soup of oh-so-comforting molecules of the physical brain. This belief will only take science so far. There seems to be little room in the fray for a quantum explanation of consciousness and for the expansion of such a consciousness on a global scale—ironically, the very notion hinted at in many of the book's discussions, albeit via a different route. Would not a shift in mass consciousness to break the bonds of staunch materialism and going deeper in a quantum no-limit future be a belief that could indeed change everything? The successful merging of materialism with advancements in the understanding of quantum mechanics is the formula for mass change.

Disappointingly missing in this book is the recognition that a uniform, specific, precise, natural, safe, and, above all, holistic set of diagnostic and treatment options for all structural, chemical, and mental ailments is what is sorely needed in the world. Many of these tools already exist; the problem lies in the vast overspecialization of most health professionals and fierce political, economic, and egotistical segregation. Fast, effective well-being delivered to the entire population of our globe will change everything.

The Energy of Belief: Psychology's Power Tools to Focus Intention and Release Blocking Beliefs

Sheila Sidney Bender, PhD, and Mary T. Sise, PhD

Energy Psychology Press, 2008
Softcover, 235 Pages
$17.95
ISBN 978-1-60415-019-3

Reviewed by Carol Crenshaw, EFT INT-1

Written on request as the layperson's self-help equivalent to a book written for professionals on the same subject, this book explains the Touch and Breathe (TAB) technique in easy-to-understand, useable terms. Written by psychologist Sheila Bender and social worker Mary Sise, the book addresses their ongoing clinical experience, which showed that negative beliefs of clients kept resurfacing over and over in different situations until the belief was finally dealt with and eliminated. TAB is their technique to eliminate these negative beliefs.

Each chapter systematically explains theory plus techniques with practice exercises. Illustrations, pictures, diagrams, and verbal directions make each technique clear and easy to use. The first five chapters teach the basics of TAB, with each chapter building on what came before. In this method, touching meridian points with mindfulness about what is happening internally is used rather than tapping the points and noting the effects. The next five chapters explain more about our energy system and how to personalize self-work by applying these principles. Chapter 11 provides a guide for developing the future you want by imagining what you want to see happen and then using your thoughts, beliefs, and intentions to bring it about. The scale used for this imagining is called SUFI (Subjective Units of Future Imagining). Chapter 12 ends with a visionary explanation of how individual inner peace impacts the peace of the world.

Although written as a self-help book, this volume is also quite useful for practitioners of energy medicine, psychologists, and other professionals. Those who already use EFT and other forms of energy psychology can build on their knowledge base with the information presented in this book. Though the basic meridian points are the same as in EFT, the order of using them and the whole sequencing of doing a round is different. This additional information is always good to have, and can be used when someone is stuck and nothing seems to be working. Especially useful are the self-test methods, which can be implemented in addition to or instead of muscle testing (to guide the treatment more accurately), simple exercises to correct disorganized polarity and neurological disorganization, charts for testing blocking beliefs (in the four major areas of safety, deservedness, concern about the future, and relationships), and a table that serves as a guide in testing for emotions, listing the corresponding meridians and where the treatment points are located. This is a book that someone could go back to again and again for fine-tuning an aspect of energy treatment, or adding it to another form of treatment.

X-ray phase-contrast CT imaging of the acupoints based on synchrotron radiation

Chenglin, L., Xiaohu, W., Hua, X., Fang, L., Ruishan, D., Dongming, Z., Xinyic, Z., Honglan, X., & Tiqiao, X.
Journal of Electron Spectroscopy and Related Phenomena (in press), published online December 30, 2013.
http://dx.doi.org/10.1016/j.elspec.2013.12.005

Abstract

In this paper, the morphology of the acupuncture point (abbreviated as acupoint hereafter) or tissue where there were no acupoints in the fractional rabbit hind limb was studied by in-line phase contrast CT imaging (PCI-CT) methods based on synchrotron radiation. The density of micro-vessels was calculated for tissues with acupoints or without acupoints. Differences between acupoints area and non-acupoint areas determined by the density of the micro-vessels propose a strong evidence of the existence of acupoints. Our results showed that there were two significantly higher densities of the micro-vessels, where two acupoints were located, respectively. In addition, there were large numbers of involutedly microvascular structure in the acupoint areas. Nevertheless, in non-acupoints area, the microvascular structure was relatively simple and flat.

The use of DC electrodermal potential measurements and healer's felt sense to assess the energetic nature of qi

Syldona, M. & Rein, G.
Journal of Alternative and Complementary Medicine (1999), 5(4), August, 329–47.
doi:10.1089/acm.1999.5.329

Abstract

Because DC electrodermal potential measurements do not involve introducing a current into the body, it was postulated that temporal fluctuations in DC potential values on acupoints would be a useful method for assessing the subtle energetic changes of qi. DC potential measurements from acupoints and nonacupoints were therefore compared when energy healing practitioners were in an external focus state, were healing at a distance (external qi), or were self-healing (internal qi). The results show statistically significant differences between measurements obtained on and off acupoints and between external focus and healing states. Subjects' report of felt sense of the flow of qi moving in their body also correlated with DC potential readings, but only those readings taken on acupoints. The results support the hypothesis that pattern information from temporal fluctuations in DC potential electrodermal measurements reflects the movement and/or amount of a physical, electrical activity that corresponds to the traditional Eastern concept of qi circulating in the body.

Is there any energy transfer during acupuncture?

Lee, M. S., Lee, Y. H., Shin, B. C., Jeong, D. M., Kim, M. K., Eo, Y. G., & Ko, S. B.

American Journal of Chinese Medicine (2005), 33(3), 507–12.
doi:10.1142/S0192415X05003107

Abstract

Acupuncture therapy is based on the principle of restoring equilibrium of the body's energy state by regulating the flow of Qi in the corresponding meridians and acupoints. The purpose of this study was to determine whether bio-energy transfer occurs during acupuncture of the meridians. We treated 20 normal healthy subjects with acupuncture and measured changes in the direct current (DC) potential between the stomach meridian points ST-39 and ST-37 in response to invasive insertion of a needle at ST-36. Using a crossover study design, the practitioner performed the procedure on each subject once with bare (uncovered) hands (ABH) and once wearing surgical gloves (ASH) to shield the electric energy transfer. ABH produced a response pattern to each stimulation, whereas ASH produced a response pattern only to the first step. ABH elicited a significantly higher response potential than did ASH ($p < 0.001$). These results suggest that there may be bio-energy (Qi) transfer during acupuncture along the meridians. This transferred bio-energy (Qi) seems to act as an electromotive force, which is purported to remove the stagnation or blockage of energy and restore an equilibrium state.

The evidence for Shiatsu: A systematic review of Shiatsu and acupressure

Robinson, N., Lorenc, A., & Liao, X.

BMC Alternative and Complementary Medicine (2011), 11(88).
http://www.biomedcentral.com/1472-6882/11/88

Background

Shiatsu, similar to acupressure, uses finger pressure, manipulations, and stretches, along traditional Chinese medicine meridians. Shiatsu is popular in Europe, but lacks reviews on its evidence base.

Methods

Acupressure and Shiatsu clinical trials were identified using the MeSH term "acupressure" in: EBM reviews, AMED, BNI, CINAHL, EMBASE, MEDLINE, PsycARTICLES, Science Direct, Blackwell Synergy, Ingenta Select, Wiley Interscience, Index to Theses, and ZETOC. References of articles were checked. Inclusion criteria were Shiatsu or acupressure administered manually/bodily, published after January 1990. Two reviewers performed independent study selection and evaluation of study design and reporting, using standardized checklists (CONSORT, TREND, CASP, and STRICTA).

Results

Searches identified 1,714 publications. Final inclusions were 9 Shiatsu and 71 acupressure studies. A quarter were graded A (highest quality). Shiatsu studies comprised 1 RCT, three controlled non-randomized, one within subjects, one observational, and 3 uncontrolled studies investigating mental and physical health issues. Evidence was of insufficient quantity and quality. Acupressure studies included 2 meta-analyses, 6 systematic reviews, and 39 RCTs. Strongest evidence was for pain (particularly dysmenorrhea, lower back, and labor), postoperative nausea, and vomiting. Additionally, quality evidence found improvements in sleep in institutionalized elderly. Variable/poor quality evidence existed for renal disease symptoms, dementia, stress, anxiety, and respiratory conditions. Appraisal tools may be inappropriate for some study designs. Potential biases included focus on UK/USA databases, limited grey literature, and exclusion of qualitative and pre-1989 studies.

Conclusions

Evidence is improving in quantity, quality, and reporting, but more research is needed, particularly for Shiatsu, where evidence is poor. Acupressure may be beneficial for pain, nausea and vomiting, and sleep.

Acupuncture for chronic pain: Individual patient data meta-analysis

Vickers, A. J., Cronin, A. M., Maschino, A. C., Lewith, G., MacPherson, H., Foster, N. E., Sherman, K. J., Witt, C. M., & Linde, K.

Archives of Internal Medicine (2012), 172(19), October 22, 1444–53.
doi:10.1001/archinternmed.2012.3654

Background

Although acupuncture is widely used for chronic pain, there remains considerable controversy as to its value. We aimed to determine the effect size of acupuncture for four chronic pain conditions: back and neck pain, osteoarthritis, chronic headache, and shoulder pain.

Methods

We conducted a systematic review to identify randomized controlled trials (RCTs) of acupuncture for chronic pain in which allocation concealment was determined unambiguously to be adequate. Individual patient data meta-analyses were conducted using data from 29 of 31 eligible RCTs, with a total of 17,922 patients analyzed.

Results

In the primary analysis, including all eligible RCTs, acupuncture was superior to both sham and no-acupuncture control for each pain condition ($P < .001$ for all comparisons). After exclusion of an outlying set of RCTs that strongly favored acupuncture, the effect sizes were similar across pain conditions. Patients receiving acupuncture had less pain, with scores that were 0.23 (95% CI, 0.13–0.33), 0.16 (95% CI, 0.07–0.25), and 0.15 (95% CI, 0.07–0.24) SDs lower than sham controls for back and neck pain, osteoarthritis, and chronic headache, respectively; the effect sizes in comparison to no-acupuncture controls were 0.55 (95% CI, 0.51–0.58), 0.57 (95% CI, 0.50–0.64), and 0.42 (95% CI, 0.37–0.46) SDs. These results were robust to a variety of sensitivity analyses, including those related to publication bias.

Conclusions

Acupuncture is effective for the treatment of chronic pain and is therefore a reasonable referral option. Significant differences between true and sham acupuncture indicate that acupuncture is more than a placebo.

German Acupuncture Trials (GERAC) for chronic low back pain: Randomized, multicenter, blinded, parallel-group trial with 3 groups

Haake, M., Müller, H. H., Schade-Brittinger, C., Basler, H. D., Schäfer, H., Maier, C., Endres, H. G., Trampisch, H. J., & Molsberger, A.

Archives of Internal Medicine (2007), 167(17), September 24, 1892–8.

Background

To our knowledge, verum acupuncture has never been directly compared with sham acupuncture and guideline-based conventional therapy in patients with chronic low back pain.

Methods

A patient- and observer-blinded randomized controlled trial conducted in Germany involving 340 outpatient practices, including 1,162 patients aged 18 to 86 years (mean +/– SD age, 50 +/– 15 years) with a history of chronic low back pain for a mean of 8 years. Patients underwent ten 30-minute sessions, generally 2 sessions per week, of verum acupuncture ($n = 387$) according to principles of traditional Chinese medicine; sham acupuncture ($n = 387$) consisting of superficial needling at nonacupuncture points; or conventional therapy, a combination of drugs, physical therapy, and exercise ($n = 388$). Five additional sessions were offered to patients who had a partial response to treatment (10%–50% reduction in pain intensity). Primary outcome was response after 6 months, defined as 33% improvement or better on three pain-related items on the Von Korff Chronic Pain Grade Scale questionnaire or 12% improvement or better on the back-specific Hanover Functional Ability Questionnaire. Patients who were unblinded or had recourse to other than permitted concomitant therapies during follow-up were classified as nonresponders regardless of symptom improvement.

Results

At 6 months, response rate was 47.6% in the verum acupuncture group, 44.2% in the sham acupuncture group, and 27.4% in the conventional therapy group. Differences among groups were as follows: verum vs. sham, 3.4% (95% confidence interval, –3.7% to 10.3%; $P = .39$); verum vs. conventional therapy, 20.2% (95% confidence interval, 13.4% to 26.7%; $P < .001$); and sham vs. conventional therapy, 16.8% (95% confidence interval, 10.1% to 23.4%; $P < .001$).

Conclusions

Low back pain improved after acupuncture treatment for at least 6 months. Effectiveness of acupuncture, either verum or sham, was almost twice that of conventional therapy.

Migraine and acupuncture: The evidence for effectiveness

Acupuncture Research Resource Centre

British Acupuncture Council (1998), June, Briefing paper #1.

http://www.acupuncture.org.uk/arrc/public-review-papers/migraine-and-acupuncture-the-evidence-for-effectiveness.html

Summary

Acupuncture has been much used in the treatment of migraine and episodic tension headache both in China and the West. This paper assesses the quantity and quality of the evidence for the use of acupuncture in treating this condition. Our conclusion is that there is some evidence that acupuncture has a significant therapeutic effect on symptoms such as pain and frequency in migraine attacks.

Conclusion

All the uncontrolled trials demonstrated that acupuncture is highly effective, often helping over 80% of patients. This is considerably more effective than a likely placebo response which has been estimated to be from around 30% to as high as 50% (Tavola, Gala, Conte, & Inverizzi, 1992). In all the controlled studies, treatment was shown to be more effective in at least one measure (i.e., pain intensity or frequency of attacks), with statistical significance reached in two studies (Vincent, 1989; Tavola et al., 1992). In the comparative study (Hesse, Movelvang, & Simonsen, 1994), acupuncture performed as well as the standard therapy with the added benefit of a lower incidence of side effects. Overall the evidence supports the hypothesis that acupuncture is effective in the treatment of migraine.

Menopause and acupuncture: The evidence for effectiveness

Acupuncture Research Resource Centre

British Acupuncture Council (1999), September, Briefing paper #5.

http://www.acupuncture.org.uk/arrc/public-review-papers/menopause-and-acupuncture-the-evidence-for-effectiveness.html

Summary

Symptoms commonly associated with the menopause are frequently treated by acupuncture (e.g., see Lyttleton, 1990a, 1991; Maciocia, 1998). This paper assesses the evidence base insofar that it is available in the literature, much of which is in French. The results of these few studies suggest that acupuncture can be effective in treating hot flushes, and also anxiety and depression related to menopause.

Conclusion

The results of the studies tend to indicate there is benefit in the use of acupuncture in the alleviation of menopausal symptoms, particularly hot flushes and anxiety.

Stroke and acupuncture: The evidence for effectiveness

Acupuncture Research Resource Centre
British Acupuncture Council (1998), June, Briefing paper #2.
http://www.acupuncture.org.uk/arrc/public-review-papers/stroke-and-acupuncture-the-evidence-for-effectiveness.html

Summary

In the West, interest in the possible effect of acupuncture on stroke has been increasing over the last 5 years with much of the recent research being carried out in the Scandinavian countries and the USA. Traditional Chinese medicine claims that the symptoms of stroke and its sequelae respond well to acupuncture treatment. Known as "wind-stroke," such treatment involves either the use body points alone, with or without electrical stimulation, or the combination of body points with scalp acupuncture (Chen, 1993). In China, many studies have compared different techniques and point combinations. Often very large numbers of patients are involved, for instance Ge (1992) treated and assessed 684 patients with sequelae of stroke at the Air Force Hospital in Shengyang.

Conclusion

There is an increase in interest in using acupuncture as a treatment modality for stroke (Ernst & White, 1996), and the recent Consensus Development Statement from a panel convened by the U.S. National Institutes of Health to consider the evidence for acupuncture (NIH, 1997) finds "positive clinical reports" for its use in this context. It would seem that the evidence to date suggests that acupuncture has a valuable role to play in helping stroke recovery.

The effectiveness of acupuncture research across components of the trauma spectrum response (tsr): A systematic review of reviews

Lee, C., Crawford, C., Wallerstedt, D., York, A., Duncan, A., Smith, J., Sprengel, M., Welton, R., & Jonas, W.

Systematic Reviews (2012), 1, October 15, 46.
doi:10.1186/2046-4053-1-46

Background

Co-morbid symptoms (for example, chronic pain, depression, anxiety, and fatigue) are particularly common in military fighters returning from the current conflicts, who have experienced physical and/or psychological trauma. These overlapping conditions cut across the boundaries of mind, brain, and body, resulting in a common symptomatic and functional spectrum of physical, cognitive, psychological and behavioral effects referred to as the "Trauma Spectrum Response" (TSR). While acupuncture has been shown to treat some of these components effectively, the current literature is often difficult to interpret, inconsistent, or of variable quality. Thus, to gauge comprehensively the effectiveness of acupuncture across TSR components, a systematic review of reviews was conducted using the Samueli Institute's Rapid Evidence Assessment of the Literature (REAL) methodology.

Methods

PubMed/MEDLINE, the Cochrane Database of Systematic Reviews, EMBASE, CINAHL, and PsycInfo were searched from inception to September 2011 for systematic reviews/meta-analyses. Quality assessment was rigorously performed using the Scottish Intercollegiate Guidelines Network (SIGN 50) checklist and the Grading of Recommendations, Assessment, Development, and Evaluation (GRADE) methodology. Adherence to the Standards for Reporting Interventions in Clinical Trials in Acupuncture (STRICTA) criteria was also assessed.

Results

Of the 1,480 citations identified by our searches, 52 systematic reviews/meta-analyses, all high quality except for one, met inclusion criteria for each TSR component except post-traumatic stress disorder (PTSD) and sexual function. The majority of reviews addressed most STRICTA components, but did not describe safety.

Conclusions

Based on the results of our review, acupuncture appears to be effective for treating headaches and, although more research is needed, seems to be a promising treatment option for anxiety, sleep disturbances, depression, and chronic pain. It does not, however, demonstrate any substantial treatment benefit for substance abuse. Because there were no reviews on PTSD or sexual function that met our pre-defined inclusion criteria, we cannot comment on acupuncture's effectiveness in treating these conditions. More quality data are also needed to determine whether acupuncture is appropriate for treating fatigue or cognitive difficulties. Further, while acupuncture has been shown to be generally safe, safety was not described in the majority of studies, making it difficult to provide any strong recommendations. Future research should address safety reporting in detail in order to increase our confidence in acupuncture's efficacy across the identified TSR components.

Acupuncture for posttraumatic stress disorder: A systematic review of randomized controlled trials and prospective clinical trials

Kim, Y-D., Heo, I., Shin, B-C., Crawford, C., Kang, H-W., & Lim, J-H.

Evidence-Based Complementary and Alternative Medicine (2013), Article ID 615857
http://dx.doi.org/10.1155/2013/615857

Abstract

To evaluate the current evidence for effectiveness of acupuncture for posttraumatic stress disorder (PTSD) in the form of a systematic review, a systematic literature search was conducted in 23 electronic databases. Grey literature was also searched. The key search terms were "acupuncture" and "PTSD." No language restrictions were imposed. We included all randomized or prospective clinical trials that evaluated acupuncture and its variants against a wait-list, sham acupuncture, conventional therapy control for PTSD, or without control. Four randomized controlled trials (RCTs) and 2 uncontrolled clinical trials (UCTs) out of 136 articles in total were systematically reviewed. One high-quality RCT reported that acupuncture was superior to waitlist control and therapeutic effects of acupuncture and cognitive-behavioral therapy (CBT) were similar based on the effect sizes. One RCT showed no statistical difference between acupuncture and selective serotonin reuptake inhibitors (SSRIs). One RCT reported a favorable effect of acupoint stimulation plus CBT against CBT alone. A meta-analysis of acupuncture plus moxibustion versus SSRI favored acupuncture plus moxibustion in three outcomes. This systematic review and meta-analysis suggests that the evidence of effectiveness of acupuncture for PTSD is encouraging but not cogent. Further qualified trials are needed to confirm whether acupuncture is effective for PTSD.

Epigenetic and immune function profiles associated with posttraumatic stress disorder

Uddin, M., Aiello, A. E., Wildman, D. E., Koenen, K. C., Pawelec, G., de Los Santos, R., Goldmann, E., & Galea, S.

Proc Natl Acad Sci U S A (2010), 107(20), May 18, 9470–5. Epub 2010, May 3.
doi:10.1073/pnas.0910794107

Abstract

The biologic underpinnings of posttraumatic stress disorder (PTSD) have not been fully elucidated. Previous work suggests that alterations in the immune system are characteristic of the disorder. Identifying the biologic mechanisms by which such alterations occur could provide fundamental insights into the etiology and treatment of PTSD. Here we identify specific epigenetic profiles underlying immune system changes associated with PTSD. Using blood samples ($n = 100$) obtained from an ongoing, prospective epidemiologic study in Detroit, the Detroit Neighborhood Health Study, we applied methylation microarrays to assay CpG sites from more than 14,000 genes among 23 PTSD-affected and 77 PTSD-unaffected individuals. We show that immune system functions are significantly overrepresented among the annotations associated with genes uniquely unmethylated among those with PTSD. We further demonstrate that genes whose methylation levels are significantly and negatively correlated with traumatic burden show a similar strong signal of immune function among the PTSD affected. The observed epigenetic variability in immune function by PTSD is corroborated using an independent biologic marker of immune response to infection, CMV—a typically latent herpesvirus whose activity was significantly higher among those with PTSD. This report of peripheral epigenomic and CMV profiles associated with mental illness suggests a biologic model of PTSD etiology in which an externally experienced traumatic event induces downstream alterations in immune function by reducing methylation levels of immune-related genes.

Childhood adversity heightens the impact of later-life caregiving stress on telomere length and inflammation

Kiecolt-Glaser, J. K., Gouin, J. P., Weng, N. P., Malarkey, W. B., Beversdorf, D. Q., & Glaser, R.

Psychosomatic Medicine (2011), 73(1), January, 16–22.

Objective

To address the question of whether childhood abuse and other adversities have lasting, detectable consequences for inflammation and cell aging late in life, and whether the effects are large enough to be discernible beyond that of a major chronic stressor, dementia family caregiving. Previous research on the physical health consequences of childhood abuse and other adversities has been based on data from young or middle-aged adults.

Method

In this community sample of 132 healthy older adults (mean age = 69.70 years; standard deviation = 10.14), including 58 dementia family caregivers and 74 non-caregivers, blood samples were analyzed for interleukin (IL)-6, tumor necrosis factor (TNF)-α, and telomere length, a measure of cell aging. Depressive symptoms were assessed by the Center for Epidemiological Studies Depression Scale.

Results

After controlling for age, caregiving status, gender, body mass index, exercise, and sleep, the presence of multiple childhood adversities was related to both heightened IL-6 (0.37 ± 0.03 log10 pg/mL versus 0.44 ± 0.03 log10 pg/mL) and shorter telomeres (6.51 ± 0.17 Kb versus 5.87 ± 0.20 Kb), compared with the absence of adversity; the telomere difference could translate into a 7- to 15-year difference in life span. Abuse was associated with heightened IL-6 and TNF-α levels; for TNF-α, this relationship was magnified in caregivers compared with controls. Moreover, abuse and caregiving status were associated significantly and independently with higher levels of depressive symptoms.

Conclusions

Adverse childhood events are related to continued vulnerability among older adults, enhancing the impact of chronic stressors. Childhood adversities cast a very long shadow.

Childhood trauma associated with short leukocyte telomere length in posttraumatic stress disorder

O'Donovan, A., Epel, E., Lin, J., Wolkowitz, O., Cohen, B., Maguen, S., Metzler, T., Lenoci, M., Blackburn, E., & Neylan, T. C.

Biological Psychiatry (2011), 70(5), September 1, 465–71. Epub 2011, April 13.
doi:10.1016/j.biopsych.2011.01.035

Background

Posttraumatic stress disorder (PTSD) is associated with increased risk for age-related diseases and early mortality. An accelerated rate of biological aging could contribute to this increased risk. To investigate, we assessed leukocyte telomere length (LTL), an emerging marker of biological age, in men and women with and without PTSD. We also examined childhood trauma, a risk factor for both PTSD and short LTL, as a potential contributor to short LTL in PTSD.

Methods

Participants included 43 adults with chronic PTSD (*n* = 18 with multiple categories of childhood trauma) and 47 control subjects (none with multiple categories of childhood trauma) (mean age = 30.55, *SD* = 7.44). Exclusion criteria included physical illness, medication use, obesity, alcohol or substance abuse, and pregnancy. Structured clinical interviews were conducted to assess PTSD and other psychiatric disorders and childhood trauma exposure. LTL was measured with a quantitative polymerase chain reaction method.

Results

As predicted, participants with PTSD had shorter age-adjusted LTL than control subjects. Exposure to childhood trauma was also associated with short LTL. In fact, childhood trauma seemed to account for the PTSD group difference in LTL; only participants with PTSD and exposure to multiple categories of childhood trauma had significantly shorter LTL than control subjects.

Conclusions

Childhood trauma is associated with short LTL in individuals with PTSD. Chronic exposure to the psychobiological sequelae of childhood trauma could increase risk for PTSD and short LTL. Thus, the lasting psychological impact of exposure to trauma in childhood might be accompanied by equally enduring changes at the molecular level.

CAM and energy psychology techniques remediate PTSD symptoms in veterans and spouses

Church, D. & Brooks, A. J.

Explore (2014), 10(1), January/February, 24–33.
http://dx.doi.org/10.1016/j.explore.2013.10.006

Abstract

Male veterans and their spouses ($N = 218$) attending one of six week-long retreats were assessed for posttraumatic stress disorder (PTSD) symptoms pre- and postintervention. Participants were evaluated using the PTSD checklist (PCL), on which, a score of >49 indicates clinical symptom levels. The mean pretest score was 61.1 ($SD \pm 12.5$) for veterans and 42.6 ($SD \pm 16.5$) for spouses; 83% of veterans and 29% of spouses met clinical criteria. The multimodal intervention used Emotional Freedom Techniques and other energy psychology (EP) methods to address PTSD symptoms and a variety of complementary and alternative medicine (CAM) modalities for stress reduction and resource building. Interventions were delivered in group format as well as individual counseling sessions. Data were analyzed for each retreat, as well as for the six retreats as a whole. Mean posttest PCL scores decreased to 41.8 ($SE \pm 1.2$; $p < .001$) for veterans, with 28% still clinical. Spouses demonstrate substantial symptom reductions ($M = 28.7$, $SE \pm 1.0$; $p < .001$), with 4% still clinical. A follow-up assessment ($n = 63$) found PTSD symptom levels dropping even further for spouses ($p < .003$), whereas gains were maintained for veterans. The significant reduction in PTSD symptoms is consistent with other published reports of EP treatment, though counter to the usual long-term course of the condition. The results indicate that a multimodal CAM intervention incorporating EP may offer benefits to family members as well as veterans suffering from PTSD symptoms. Recommendations are made for further research to answer the questions posed by this study.

Prevalence of delayed-onset posttraumatic stress disorder in military personnel: Is there evidence for this disorder? Results of a prospective UK cohort study

Goodwin, L., Jones, M., Rona, R. J., Sundin, J., Wessely, S., & Fear, N. T.

Journal of Nervous and Mental Disease (2012), 200(5), May, 429–37.
doi:10.1097/NMD.0b013e31825322fe

Abstract

Delayed-onset posttraumatic stress disorder (PTSD) is defined as onset at least 6 months after a traumatic event. This study investigates the prevalence of delayed-onset PTSD in 1397 participants from a two-phase prospective cohort study of UK military personnel. Delayed-onset PTSD was categorized as participants who did not meet the criteria for probable PTSD (assessed using the PTSD Checklist Civilian version) at phase 1 but met the criteria by phase 2. Of the participants, 3.5% met the criteria for delayed-onset PTSD. Subthreshold PTSD, common mental disorder (CMD), poor/fair self-reported health, and multiple physical symptoms at phase 1 and the onset of alcohol misuse or CMD between phases 1 and 2 were associated with delayed-onset PTSD. Delayed-onset PTSD exists in this UK military sample. Military personnel who developed delayed-onset PTSD were more likely to have psychological ill-health at an earlier assessment, and clinicians should be aware of the potential comorbidity in these individuals, including alcohol misuse. Leaving the military or experiencing relationship breakdown was not associated.

Posttraumatic stress disorder is associated with an enhanced spontaneous production of pro-inflammatory cytokines by peripheral blood mononuclear cells

Gola, H., Engler, H., Sommershof, A., Adenauer, H., Kolassa, S., Schedlowski, M., Groettrup, M., Elbert, T., & Kolassa, I-T.

BMC Psychiatry (2013), 13, January 29, 40.
doi:10.1186/1471-244X-13-40

Background

Posttraumatic stress disorder (PTSD) is associated with an enhanced risk for cardiovascular and other inflammatory diseases. Chronic low-level inflammation has been suggested as a potential mechanism linking these conditions.

Methods

We investigated plasma cytokine levels as well as spontaneous and lipopolysaccharide (LPS)-stimulated cytokine production by peripheral blood mononuclear cells (PBMCs) in a group of 35 severely traumatized PTSD patients compared to 25 healthy controls.

Results

Spontaneous production of interleukin (IL)-1β, IL-6 and tumor necrosis factor (TNF)-α by isolated PBMCs was significantly higher in the PTSD compared to the control group and even correlated with PTSD symptom severity within the PTSD group. In contrast, circulating plasma levels of pro- and anti-inflammatory cytokines such as IL-6, IL-8, IL-10, TNF-α, or monocyte chemotactic protein (MCP)-1 were not significantly altered in PTSD patients compared to healthy controls.

Conclusions

Our findings indicate that PBMCs of PTSD patients are already pre-activated in vivo, providing further evidence for low-grade inflammation in PTSD. This might possibly represent one psychobiological pathway from PTSD to poor physical health.

EMDR therapy: An overview of current and future research

Shapiro, F.
European Review of Applied Psychology (2012), 62(4), October, 193–5.
http://dx.doi.org/10.1016/j.erap.2012.09.005

Introduction

EMDR therapy is an eight-phase treatment approach widely recognized as a frontline treatment for trauma. Research over the past decade has addressed the utility of the eye movements, mechanism of action, and comparisons with other forms of therapy.

Literature and clinical findings

More than two-dozen randomized controlled trials (RCT) demonstrate the positive effects of EMDR therapy with trauma victims. Comparisons with trauma-focused cognitive behavioral therapy (TF-CBT) indicate comparable effects sizes. Approximately 20 additional RCT evaluated the eye movement component of EMDR in isolation, without the rest of the therapy procedures. These studies document a variety of positive effects, including a rapid decrease in distress and reduced clarity of the targeted disturbing image when compared to exposure-only conditions.

Discussion

Research findings indicate that EMDR therapy and TF-CBT are based on different mechanisms of action in that EMDR therapy does not necessitate daily homework, sustained arousal, or detailed descriptions of the event, and appears to take fewer sessions. EMDR is guided by the adaptive information-processing model, which posits a wide range of adverse life experiences as the basis of pathology.

Conclusions

Research is suggested to further explore mechanisms of action and address issues of efficiency and treatment differences. Rigorous research is also needed to investigate additional clinical applications.

Psychological treatments for chronic post-traumatic stress disorder: Systematic review and meta-analysis

Bisson, J. I., Ehlers, A., Matthews, R., Pilling, S., Richards, D., & Turner, S.

British Journal of Psychiatry (2007), 190, 97–104.
doi:10.1192/bjp.bp.106.021402

Background

The relative efficacy of different psychological treatments for chronic post-traumatic stress disorder (PTSD) is unclear.

Aims

To determine the efficacy of specific psychological treatments for chronic PTSD.

Method

In a systematic review of randomized controlled trials, eligible studies were assessed against methodological quality criteria and data were extracted and analyzed.

Results

Thirty-eight randomized controlled trials were included in the meta-analysis. Trauma-focused cognitive-behavioral therapy (TFCBT), eye movement desensitization and reprocessing (EMDR), stress management and group cognitive-behavioral therapy improved PTSD symptoms more than waiting-list or usual care. There was inconclusive evidence regarding other therapies. There was no evidence of a difference in efficacy between TFCBT and EMDR but there was some evidence that TFCBT and EMDR were superior to stress management and other therapies, and that stress management was superior to other therapies.

Conclusions

The first-line psychological treatment for PTSD should be trauma-focused (TFCBT or EMDR).

Cognitive behavior therapy versus eye movement desensitization and reprocessing for post-traumatic disorder—is it all in the homework then?

Ho, M. S. K. & Lee, C. W.

European Review of Applied Psychology (2012), 62(4), 253–60.
http://dx.doi.org/10.1016/j.erap.2012.08.001

Introduction

Treatment of choice for post-traumatic stress disorder (PTSD) is either eye movement desensitization and reprocessing (EMDR) or trauma-focused cognitive behavior therapy (TFCBT).

Objective

The aim of the present meta-analysis was to determine whether there are any differences between these two treatments with respect to efficacy and efficiency in treating PTSD.

Method

We performed a comprehensive literature search using several electronic search engines as well as manual searches of other review papers. Eight original studies involving 227 participants were identified in this manner.

Results

There were no differences between EMDR and TFCBT on measures of PTSD. However, there was a significant advantage for EMDR over TFCBT in reducing depression (Hedges' $g = 0.63$). The analysis also indicated a difference in the prescribed homework between the treatments. Meta-regression analyses were conducted to examine the relationship between hours of homework and gains in depression and PTSD symptoms.

Conclusion

These findings are discussed in terms of efficacy and cost-effectiveness and the use of homework in therapy.

Control of stress-induced persistent anxiety by an extra-amygdala septohypothalamic circuit

Anthony, T. E., Dee, N., Bernard, A., Lerchner, W., Heintz, N., & Anderson, D. J.

Cell (2014), 156(3), 522–36.

Abstract

The extended amygdala has dominated research on the neural circuitry of fear and anxiety, but the septohippocampal axis also plays an important role. The lateral septum (LS) is thought to suppress fear and anxiety through its outputs to the hypothalamus. However, this structure has not yet been dissected using modern tools. The type 2 CRF receptor (Crfr2) marks a subset of LS neurons whose functional connectivity we have investigated using optogenetics. Crfr2+ cells include GABAergic projection neurons that connect with the anterior hypothalamus. Surprisingly, we find that these LS outputs enhance stress-induced behavioral measures of anxiety. Furthermore, transient activation of Crfr2+ neurons promotes, while inhibition suppresses, persistent anxious behaviors. LS Crfr2+ outputs also positively regulate circulating corticosteroid levels. These data identify a subset of LS projection neurons that promote, rather than suppress, stress-induced behavioral and endocrinological dimensions of persistent anxiety states and provide a cellular point of entry to LS circuitry.

Elevated morning cortisol is a stratified population-level biomarker for major depression in boys only with high depressive symptoms

Owens, M., Herbert, J., Jones, P. B., Sahakian, B. J., Wilkinson, P. O., Dunn, V. J., Croudace, T. J., & Goodyer, I. M.

Proc Natl Acad Sci U S A (2014), 111(9), March 4, 3638–43. Epub 2014, February 18.
doi:10.1073/pnas.1318786111

Abstract

Clinical depression is a severe and common illness, characterized primarily by persistent low mood and lack of pleasure in usually enjoyable activities, that results in significant impairment in everyday living. It also involves alterations in cognitive and hormonal functions. There is substantial variation between depressed individuals in terms of the causes and therapeutic response, making it difficult to identify those most likely to benefit from intervention and treatment. We derived subtypes of adolescents in the population based on different levels of the hormone cortisol and subclinical depressive symptoms. A group (17%) with both high levels of cortisol and depressive symptoms of both sexes had more depressed thinking. Boys in this group were at high risk for clinical depression.

Dehydroepiandrosterone (DHEA) treatment of depression

Wolkowitz, O. M., Reus, V. I., Roberts, E., Manfredi, F., Chan, T., Raum, W. J., Ormiston, S., Johnson, R., Canick, J., Brizendine, L., & Weingartner, H.

Biological Psychiatry (1997), 41(3), February 1, 311–8.

Abstract

Dehydroepiandrosterone (DHEA) and its sulfate, DHEA-S, are plentiful adrenal steroid hormones that decrease with aging and may have significant neuropsychiatric effects. In this study, six middle-aged and elderly patients with major depression and low basal plasma DHEA f1p4or DHEA-S levels were openly administered DHEA (30–90 mg/d × 4 weeks) in doses sufficient to achieve circulating plasma levels observed in younger healthy individuals. Depression ratings as well as aspects of memory performance significantly improved. One treatment-resistant patient received extended treatment with DHEA for 6 months: her depression ratings improved 48–72% and her semantic memory performance improved 63%. These measures returned to baseline after treatment ended. In both studies, improvements in depression ratings and memory performance were directly related to increases in plasma levels of DHEA and DHEA-S and to increases in their ratios with plasma cortisol levels. These preliminary data suggest DHEA may have antidepressant and pro-memory effects and should encourage double-blind trials in depressed patients.

A PET study following treatment with a pharmacological stressor, FG7142, in conscious rhesus monkeys

Takamatsu, H., Noda, A., Kurumaji, A., Murakami, Y., Tatsumi, M., Ichise, R., & Nishimura, S.

Brain Research (2003), 980(2), August 8, 275–80.
http://dx.doi.org/10.1016/S0006-8993(03)02987-1

Abstract

FG7142 is a benzodiazepine partial inverse agonist, which is known as a pharmacological stressor. Several reports demonstrated that FG7142 produced anxiety in humans, non-human primates, and rodents, and impaired working memory in non-human primates and rodents. In this study, we examined the effect of FG7142 on cerebral blood flow and glucose metabolism using positron emission tomography (PET) in conscious rhesus monkeys. Male rhesus monkeys were intramuscularly treated with FG7142 (0.2 or 1.0 mg/kg, $n = 5$, respectively), and regional cerebral blood flow (rCBF) and regional cerebral metabolic rate of glucose (rCMRglc) were measured by PET 20 minutes and 40 minutes after treatment, respectively. During PET measurement, physiological parameters and plasma cortisol levels were monitored. FG7142 significantly decreased rCBF in the thalamus and rCMRglc in all brain regions examined in a dose-dependent manner without changes in physiological parameters. FG7142 also significantly increased plasma cortisol levels. The present study may provide an important insight into the understanding of the pathophysiology of anxiety and stress-related disorders in humans, and strongly suggesting that prevention of anxiety or stress is important when measuring conscious brain function.

A PET study after treatment with an anxiety-provoking agent, m-chlorophenyl-piperazine, in conscious rhesus monkeys

Takamatsu, H., Noda, A., Murakami, Y., Tatsumi, M., Ichise, R., & Nishimura, S.

Journal of Nuclear Medicine (2003), 44(9), 1516–21.

Abstract

Several PET studies have been performed on conscious nonhuman primates to examine brain function. However, it is unclear how anxiety or stress during PET measurements influences brain function. In the present study, we examined the effects of a well-known anxiety-provoking agent, m-chlorophenyl-piperazine (mCPP), on regional cerebral blood flow (rCBF) and the regional cerebral metabolic rate of glucose (rCMRglc) using PET on conscious rhesus monkeys.

Methods

Male rhesus monkeys with experience undergoing PET measurements were used. Twenty and 40 minutes after mCPP injection (0.2, 1.0, or 5.0 mg/kg intramuscularly; $n = 5$), rCBF and rCMRglc were measured using an intravenous injection of 15O-H_2O and 18F-FDG, respectively. Physiologic parameters, plasma cortisol, and prolactin levels were monitored during PET measurements.

Results

Treatment with mCPP significantly increased rCBF in both the cingulate cortex and striatum in a dose-dependent manner, and bell-shaped reductions in rCMRglc were observed for all regions examined. mCPP also significantly increased plasma cortisol and prolactin levels. Physiologic parameters were not affected by mCPP treatment.

Conclusion

The present study demonstrates that treatment with the anxiety-provoking agent mCPP significantly affects rCBF and rCMRglc in conscious monkeys. Therefore, since the increases in hormone levels demonstrate that mCPP treatment produced anxiety or stress, these results suggest that anxiety or stress influences conscious brain function. Furthermore, the present study suggests that prevention of anxiety or stress is important when measuring conscious brain function in monkeys.

Noise stress impairs prefrontal cortical cognitive function in monkeys: Evidence for a hyperdopaminergic mechanism

Arnsten, A. F. & Goldman-Rakic, P. S.

Archives of General Psychiatry (1998), 55(4), 362–8.

Background

Stress can exacerbate a number of psychiatric disorders, many of which are associated with prefrontal cortical (PFC) cognitive deficits. Biochemical studies demonstrate that mild stress preferentially increases dopamine turnover in the PFC. Our study examined the effects of acute, mild stress exposure on higher cognitive function in monkeys, and the role of dopaminergic mechanisms in the stress response.

Methods

The effects of loud (105-dB) noise stress were examined on a spatial working memory task (delayed response) dependent on the PFC, and on a reference memory task with similar motor and motivational demands (visual pattern discrimination) dependent on the inferior temporal cortex. The role of dopamine mechanisms was tested by challenging the stress response with agents that decrease dopamine receptor stimulation.

Results

Exposure to noise stress significantly impaired delayed-response performance. Stress did not impair performance on "0-second" delay control trials and did not alter visual pattern discrimination performance, which is consistent with impaired PFC cognitive function rather than nonspecific changes in performance. Stress-induced deficits in delayed-response performance were ameliorated by pretreatment with drugs that block dopamine receptors (haloperidol, SCH 23390) or reduce stress-induced PFC dopamine turnover in rodents (clonidine, naloxone hydrochloride).

Conclusions

These results indicate that stress impairs PFC cognitive function through a hyperdopaminergic mechanism. Stress may take the PFC "off-line" to allow more habitual responses mediated by posterior cortical and subcortical structures to regulate behavior. This mechanism may have survival value, but may often be maladaptive in human society, contributing to the vulnerability of the PFC in many neuropsychiatric disorders.

Smaller hippocampal volume predicts pathologic vulnerability to psychological trauma

Gilbertson, M. W., Shenton, M. E., Ciszewski, A., Kasai, K., Lasko, N. B., Orr, S. P., & Pitman, R. K.

Nature Neuroscience (2002), 5, 1242–7.
doi:10.1038/nn958

Abstract

In animals, exposure to severe stress can damage the hippocampus. Recent human studies show smaller hippocampal volume in individuals with the stress-related psychiatric condition posttraumatic stress disorder (PTSD). Does this represent the neurotoxic effect of trauma, or is smaller hippocampal volume a preexisting condition that renders the brain more vulnerable to the development of pathological stress responses? In monozygotic twins discordant for trauma exposure, we found evidence that smaller hippocampi indeed constitute a risk factor for the development of stress-related psychopathology. Disorder severity in PTSD patients who were exposed to trauma was negatively correlated with the hippocampal volume of both the patients and the patients' trauma-unexposed identical co-twin. Furthermore, severe PTSD twin pairs—both the trauma-exposed and unexposed members—had significantly smaller hippocampi than non-PTSD pairs.

The nocebo phenomenon: Concept, evidence, and implications for public health

Hahn, R. A.

Preventive Medicine (1997), 26(5 Pt 1), September–October, 607–11.

Abstract

The nocebo hypothesis proposes that expectations of sickness and the affective states associated with such expectations cause sickness in the expectant. The nocebo phenomenon is a little-recognized facet of culture that may be responsible for a substantial variety of pathology throughout the world. However, the extent of the phenomenon is not yet known, and evidence is piecemeal and ambiguous. This paper reviews the concept of nocebo and its association with the placebo phenomenon, gives examples of evidence for the nocebo phenomenon, and suggests public health implications.

Epigenetic inheritance and the intergenerational transfer of experience

Harper, L. V.

Psychological Bulletin (2005), 131(3), 340–60.

Abstract

Currently, behavioral development is thought to result from the interplay among genetic inheritance, congenital characteristics, cultural contexts, and parental practices as they directly impact the individual. Evolutionary ecology points to another contributor, epigenetic inheritance, the transmission to offspring of parental phenotypic responses to environmental challenges, even when the young do not experience the challenges themselves. Genetic inheritance is not altered, gene expression is. Organismic pathways for such transmission exist. Maternal stress during the latter half of a daughter's gestation may affect not only the daughter's but also grand-offspring's physical growth. The author argues that temperamental variation may be influenced in the same way. Implications for theory and research design are presented along with testable predictions.

Rapid changes in histone deacetylases and inflammatory gene expression in expert meditators

Kaliman, P., Álvarez-López, M. J., Cosín-Tomás, M., Rosenkranz, M. A., Lutz, A., & Davidson, R. J.
Psychoneuroendocrinology (2014), 40, February, 96–107. Epub 2013, November 15.
doi:10.1016/j.psyneuen.2013.11.004

Background

A growing body of research shows that mindfulness meditation can alter neural, behavioral, and biochemical processes. However, the mechanisms responsible for such clinically relevant effects remain elusive.

Methods

Here we explored the impact of a day of intensive practice of mindfulness meditation in experienced subjects ($n = 19$) on the expression of circadian, chromatin modulatory, and inflammatory genes in peripheral blood mononuclear cells (PBMC). In parallel, we analyzed a control group of subjects with no meditation experience who engaged in leisure activities in the same environment ($n = 21$). PBMC from all participants were obtained before (t1) and after (t2) the intervention (t2–t1 = 8 h) and gene expression was analyzed using custom pathway focused quantitative-real time PCR assays. Both groups were also presented with the Trier Social Stress Test (TSST).

Results

Core clock gene expression at baseline (t1) was similar between groups and their rhythmicity was not influenced in meditators by the intensive day of practice. Similarly, we found that all the epigenetic regulatory enzymes and inflammatory genes analyzed exhibited similar basal expression levels in the two groups. In contrast, after the brief intervention we detected reduced expression of histone deacetylase genes (HDAC 2, 3 and 9), alterations in global modification of histones (H4ac; H3K4me3) and decreased expression of pro-inflammatory genes (RIPK2 and COX2) in meditators compared with controls. We found that the expression of RIPK2 and HDAC2 genes was associated with a faster cortisol recovery to the TSST in both groups.

Conclusions

The regulation of HDACs and inflammatory pathways may represent some of the mechanisms underlying the therapeutic potential of mindfulness-based interventions. Our findings set the foundation for future studies to further assess meditation strategies for the treatment of chronic inflammatory conditions.

Pessimism correlates with leukocyte telomere shortness and elevated interleukin-6 in postmenopausal women

O'Donovan, A., Lin, J., Tillie, J., Dhabhar, F. S., Wolkowitz, O. M., Blackburn, E. H., & Epel, E. S.

Brain, Behavior, and Immunity (2009), 23(4), May, 446–9. Epub 2008, December 11.
doi:10.1016/j.bbi.2008.11.006

Abstract

The combination of less positive and more negative expectations for the future (i.e., lower optimism and higher pessimism) increases risk for disease and early mortality. We tested the possibility that expectancies might influence health outcomes by altering the rate of biological aging, specifically of the immune system (immunosenescence). However, no studies to date have examined associations between optimism or pessimism and indicators of immunosenescence such as leukocyte telomere length (TL) and interleukin-6 (IL-6) levels. We investigated whether dispositional tendencies toward optimism and pessimism were associated with TL and IL-6 in a sample of 36 healthy post-menopausal women. Multiple regression analyses where optimism and pessimism were entered simultaneously, and chronological age and caregiver status were controlled, indicated that pessimism was independently associated with shorter TL ($\beta = -.68$, $p = .001$) and higher IL-6 concentrations ($\beta = .50$, $p = .02$). In contrast, optimism was not independently associated with either measure of immunosenescence. These findings suggest that dispositional pessimism may increase IL-6 and accelerate rate of telomere shortening. Mechanistic causal relationships between these parameters need to be investigated.

The power of exercise: Buffering the effect of chronic stress on telomere length

Puterman, E., Lin, J., Blackburn, E., O'Donovan, A., Adler, N., & Epel, E.

PloS One (2010), 5(5), May 26, e10837.
doi:10.1371/journal.pone.0010837

Background

Chronic psychological stress is associated with detrimental effects on physical health, and may operate in part through accelerated cell aging, as indexed by shorter telomeres at the ends of chromosomes. However, not all people under stress have distinctly short telomeres, and we examined whether exercise can serve a stress-buffering function. We predicted that chronic stress would be related to short telomere length (TL) in sedentary individuals, whereas in those who exercise, stress would not have measurable effects on telomere shortening.

Methodology and principal findings

63 healthy post-menopausal women underwent a fasting morning blood draw for whole blood TL analysis by a quantitative polymerase chain reaction method. Participants completed the Perceived Stress Scale (Cohen, Kamarck, & Mermelstein, 1983), and for 3 successive days reported daily minutes of vigorous activity. Participants were categorized into two groups—sedentary and active (those getting Centers for Disease Control–recommended daily amount of activity). The likelihood of having short versus long telomeres was calculated as a function of stress and exercise group, covarying age, BMI, and education. Logistic regression analyses revealed a significant moderating effect of exercise. As predicted, among non-exercisers a 1 unit increase in the Perceived Stress Scale was related to a 15-fold increase in the odds of having short telomeres ($p < .05$), whereas in exercisers, perceived stress appears to be unrelated to TL ($B = -.59$, $SE = .78$, $p = .45$).

Discussion

Vigorous physical activity appears to protect those experiencing high stress by buffering its relationship with TL. We propose pathways through which physical activity acts to buffer stress effects.

Cumulative inflammatory load is associated with short leukocyte telomere length in the Health, Aging, and Body Composition Study

O'Donovan, A., Pantell, M. S., Puterman, E., Dhabhar, F. S., Blackburn, E. H., Yaffe, K., Cawthon, R. M., Opresko, P. L., Hsueh, W-C., Satterfield, S., Newman, A. B., Ayonayon, H. N., Rubin, S. M., Harris, T. B., & Epel, E. S.

PloS One (2011), 6(5), e19687. Epub 2011, May 13.
doi:10.1371/journal.pone.0019687

Background

Leukocyte telomere length (LTL) is an emerging marker of biological age. Chronic inflammatory activity is commonly proposed as a promoter of biological aging in general, and of leukocyte telomere shortening in particular. In addition, senescent cells with critically short telomeres produce pro-inflammatory factors. However, in spite of the proposed causal links between inflammatory activity and LTL, there is little clinical evidence in support of their covariation and interaction.

Methodology/Principal findings

To address this issue, we examined if individuals with high levels of the systemic inflammatory markers interleukin-6 (IL-6), tumor necrosis factor-α (TNF-α), and C-reactive protein (CRP) had increased odds for short LTL. Our sample included 1,962 high-functioning adults who participated in the Health, Aging, and Body Composition Study (age range: 70–79 years). Logistic regression analyses indicated that individuals with high levels of either IL-6 or TNF-α had significantly higher odds for short LTL. Furthermore, individuals with high levels of both IL-6 and TNF-α had significantly higher odds for short LTL compared with those who had neither high ($OR = 0.52$, CI = 0.37–0.72), only IL-6 high ($OR = 0.57$, CI = 0.39–0.83) or only TNF-α high ($OR = 0.67$, CI = 0.46–0.99), adjusting for a wide variety of established risk factors and potential confounds. In contrast, CRP was not associated with LTL.

Conclusions/Significance

Results suggest that cumulative inflammatory load, as indexed by the combination of high levels of IL-6 and TNF-α, is associated with increased odds for short LTL. In contrast, high levels of CRP were not accompanied by short LTL in this cohort of older adults. These data provide the first large-scale demonstration of links between inflammatory markers and LTL in an older population.

Stress appraisals and cellular aging: A key role for anticipatory threat in the relationship between psychological stress and telomere length

O'Donovan, A., Tomiyama, A. J., Lin, J., Puterman, E., Adler, N. E., Kemeny, M., Wolkowitz, O. M., Blackburn, E. H., & Epel, E. S.

Brain, Behavior, and Immunity (2012), 26(4), May, 573–9. Epub 2012, January 24.
doi:10.1016/j.bbi.2012.01.007

Abstract

Chronic psychological stress is a risk factor for multiple diseases of aging. Accelerated cellular aging as indexed by short telomere length has emerged as a potential common biological mechanism linking various forms of psychological stress and diseases of aging. Stress appraisals determine the degree and type of biological stress responses and altered stress appraisals may be a common psychological mechanism linking psychological stress and diseases of aging. However, no previous studies have examined the relationship between stress appraisals and telomere length. We exposed chronically stressed female caregivers and non-caregiving controls ($N = 50$; M age = 62.14 ± 6.10) to a standardized acute laboratory stressor and measured their anticipatory and retrospective threat and challenge appraisals of the stressor. We hypothesized that threat and challenge appraisals would be associated with shorter and longer telomere length respectively, and that chronic caregiving stress would influence telomere length through altered stress appraisals. Higher anticipatory threat appraisals were associated with shorter age-adjusted telomere length ($\beta = -.32$, $p = .03$), but challenge appraisals and retrospective threat appraisals showed no independent association with telomere length. Caregivers reported significantly higher anticipatory ($\beta = -.36$, $p = .006$) and retrospective ($\beta = -.29$, $p = .03$) threat appraisals than controls, but similar challenge appraisals. Although there was no significant main effect of caregiver status on telomere length, caregiving had a significant indirect effect on telomere length through anticipatory threat appraisals. Exaggerated anticipatory threat appraisals may be a common and modifiable psychological mechanism of psychological stress effects on cellular aging.

Does cellular aging relate to patterns of allostasis? An examination of basal and stress reactive HPA axis activity and telomere length

Tomiyama, A. J., O'Donovan, A., Lin, J., Puterman, E., Lazaro, A., Chan, J., Dhabhar, F. S., Wolkowitz, O., Kirschbaum, C., Blackburn, E., & Epel, E.

Physiology and Behavior (2012), 106(1), April 12, 40–5. Epub 2011, November 28.
doi:10.1016/j.physbeh.2011.11.016

Abstract

Long-term exposure to stress and its physiological mediators, in particular cortisol, may lead to impaired telomere maintenance. In this study, we examine if greater cortisol responses to an acute stressor and/or dysregulated patterns of daily cortisol secretion are associated with shorter telomere length. Twenty-three postmenopausal women comprising caregivers for dementia partners ($n = 14$) and age- and BMI-matched non-caregivers provided home sampling of cortisol-saliva samples at waking, 30 minutes after waking, and bedtime, and a 12-hour overnight urine collection. They were also exposed to an acute laboratory stressor throughout which they provided saliva samples. Peripheral blood mononuclear cells were isolated from a fasting blood sample and assayed for telomere length. As hypothesized, greater cortisol responses to the acute stressor were associated with shorter telomeres, as were higher overnight urinary free cortisol levels and flatter daytime cortisol slopes. While robust physiological responses to acute stress serve important functions, the long-term consequences of frequent high stress reactivity may include accelerated telomere shortening.

Improved in situ detection method for telomeric tandem repeats in metaphase spreads and interphase nuclei

Uhlmann, V., Prasad, M., Silva, I., Luettich, K., Grande, L., Alonso, L., Thisted, M., Pluzek, K. J., Gorst, J., Ring, M., Sweeney, M., Kenny, C., Martin, C., Russell, J., Bermingham, N., O'Donovan, M., Sheils, O., & O'Leary, J. J.
Molecular Pathology (2000), 53(1), February, 48–50.

Abstract

Peptide nucleic acid technology (PNA) has become an extremely useful tool and promises to impact on molecular biology and diagnostics. These synthetic DNA analogues pair with DNA and RNA molecules according to Watson and Crick base pairing rules. This paper describes a sensitive and quick fluorescent in situ hybridization (ISH) technique to determine DNA telomere repeat sequences (TTA GGG)n using epifluorescence microscopy. Telomeres are special, repeated structures at the end of each eukaryotic chromosome and serve as protective caps to prevent DNA rearrangements and fusion of chromosomes. A model system has been developed, using stimulated peripheral blood lymphocytes, which facilitates simultaneous detection of telomeres in metaphase as well as in interphase nuclei. A fluorescein isothiocyanate labeled PNA probe (18 mer) directed against complementary telomeric sequences at the end of each chromosome is used. In addition, a simple, easy to perform PNA-ISH protocol is described that overcomes common hybridization problems encountered using DNA and RNA oligoprobes. Furthermore, the usefulness of a chromogenic immunocytochemical detection system is shown for PNA-ISH.

Shorter leukocyte telomere length in midlife women with poor sleep quality

Prather, A. A., Puterman, E., Lin, J., O'Donovan, A., Krauss, J., Tomiyama, A. J., Epel, E. S., & Blackburn, E. H.
Journal of Aging Research (2011), 2011, 721390. Epub 2011, October 20.
doi:10.4061/2011/721390.

Background

Accumulating evidence supports leukocyte telomere length (LTL) as a biological marker of cellular aging. Poor sleep is a risk factor for age-related disease; however, the extent to which sleep accounts for variation in LTL is unknown.

Methods

The present study examined associations of self-reported sleep duration, onset latency, and subjective quality with LTL in a community-dwelling sample of 245 healthy women in midlife (aged 49–66 years).

Results

While sleep duration and onset latency were unrelated to LTL, women reporting poorer sleep quality displayed shorter LTL ($r = 0.14$, $P = 0.03$), independent of age, BMI, race, and income ($b = 55.48$, $SE = 27.43$, $P = 0.04$). When analyses were restricted to participants for whom sleep patterns were chronic, poorer sleep quality predicted shorter LTL independent of covariates and perceived psychological stress.

Conclusions

This study provides the first evidence that poor sleep quality explains significant variation in LTL, a marker of cellular aging.

Mutations in the selenocysteine insertion sequence-binding protein 2 gene lead to a multisystem selenoprotein deficiency disorder in humans

Schoenmakers, E., Agostini, M., Mitchell, C., Schoenmakers, N., Papp, L., Rajanayagam, O., Padidela, R., Ceron-Gutierrez, L., Doffinger, R., Prevosto, C., Luan, J., Montano, S., Lu, J., Castanet, M., Clemons, N., Groeneveld, M., Castets, P., Karbaschi, M., Aitken, S., Dixon, A., Williams, J., Campi, I., Blount, M., Burton, H., Muntoni, F., O'Donovan, D., Dean, A., Warren, A., Brierley, C., Baguley, D., Guicheney, P., Fitzgerald, R., Coles, A., Gaston, H., Todd, P., Holmgren, A., Khanna, K. K., Cooke, M., Semple, R., Halsall, D., Wareham, N., Schwabe, J., Grasso, L., Beck-Peccoz, P., Ogunko, A., Dattani, M., Gurnell, M., & Chatterjee, K.

Journal of Clinical Investigation (2010), 120(12), December, 4220–35. Epub 2010, November 15.
doi:10.1172/JCI43653

Abstract

Selenium, a trace element that is fundamental to human health, is incorporated into some proteins as selenocysteine (Sec), generating a family of selenoproteins. Sec incorporation is mediated by a multiprotein complex that includes Sec insertion sequence-binding protein 2 (SECISBP2; also known as SBP2). Here, we describe subjects with compound heterozygous defects in the SECISBP2 gene. These individuals have reduced synthesis of most of the 25 known human selenoproteins, resulting in a complex phenotype. Azoospermia, with failure of the latter stages of spermatogenesis, was associated with a lack of testis-enriched selenoproteins. An axial muscular dystrophy was also present, with features similar to myopathies caused by mutations in selenoprotein N (SEPN1). Cutaneous deficiencies of antioxidant selenoenzymes, increased cellular ROS, and susceptibility to ultraviolet radiation-induced oxidative damage may mediate the observed photosensitivity. Reduced levels of selenoproteins in peripheral blood cells were associated with impaired T lymphocyte proliferation, abnormal mononuclear cell cytokine secretion, and telomere shortening. Paradoxically, raised ROS in affected subjects was associated with enhanced systemic and cellular insulin sensitivity, similar to findings in mice lacking the antioxidant selenoenzyme glutathione peroxidase 1 (GPx1). Thus, mutation of SECISBP2 is associated with a multisystem disorder with defective biosynthesis of many selenoproteins, highlighting their role in diverse biological processes.

Carcinogen-specific mutational and epigenetic alterations in INK4A, INK4B and p53 tumour-suppressor genes drive induced senescence bypass in normal diploid mammalian cells

Yasaei, H., Gilham, E., Pickles, J. C., Roberts, T. P., O'Donovan, M., & Newbold, R. F.
Oncogene (2013), 32(2), January 10, 171–9. Epub 2012, March 12.
doi:10.1038/onc.2012.45

Abstract

Immortalization (senescence bypass) is a critical rate-limiting step in the malignant transformation of mammalian somatic cells. Human cells must breach at least two distinct senescence barriers to permit unfettered clonal evolution during cancer development: (1) stress- or oncogene-induced premature senescence (SIPS/OIS), mediated via the p16-Rb and/or ARF-p53-p21 tumour-suppressive pathways; and (2) replicative senescence triggered by telomere shortening. In contrast, because their telomerase is constitutively active, cells from small rodents possess only the SIPS/OIS barrier, and are therefore useful for studying SIPS/OIS bypass in isolation. Dermal fibroblasts from the Syrian hamster (SHD cells) are exceptionally resistant to spontaneous SIPS bypass, but it can be readily induced following exposure to a wide range of chemical and physical carcinogens. Here we show that a spectrum of carcinogen-specific mutational and epigenetic alterations involving the INK4A (p16), p53 and INK4B (p15) genes are associated with induced SIPS bypass. With ionizing radiation, immortalization is invariably accompanied by efficient biallelic deletion of the complete INK4/CDKN2 locus. In comparison, SHD cells immortalized by the powerful polycyclic hydrocarbon carcinogen benzo(a)pyrene display transversion point mutations in the DNA-binding domain of p53 coupled with INK4 alterations such as loss of expression of p15. Epimutational silencing of p16 is the primary event associated with immortalization by nickel, a human non-genotoxic carcinogen. As SIPS/OIS bypass is a prerequisite for the immortalization of normal diploid human epithelial cells, our results with the SHD model will provide a basis for delineating combinations of key molecular changes underpinning this important event in human carcinogenesis.

Prenatal maternal cortisol levels and infant behavior during the first 5 months

De Weerth, C., van Hees, Y., & Buitelaar, J. K.
Early Human Development (2003), 74(2), November, 139–51.

Background and aims

Research on both animals and humans is providing more and more evidence that prenatal factors can have long-term effects on development. Most human studies have examined the effects of prenatal stress on birth outcome (i.e., shorter pregnancies, smaller infants). The few studies that have looked at the infants' later development have found prenatal stress to be related to more difficult temperament, behavioral/emotional problems, and poorer motor/cognitive development. In this paper, we have examined links between late pregnancy cortisol levels and infant behavior during the first 5 months of life.

Study design and subjects

Seventeen mothers and their healthy, full-term infants participated in this prospective, longitudinal study. The mothers' cortisol was determined in late pregnancy. The infants' behavior was videotaped during a series of bath sessions at the home: at 1, 3, 5, 7, 18, and 20 weeks of age. The mothers filled in temperament questionnaires (ICQ) in postnatal weeks 7 and 18.

Results and conclusions

The infants were divided into two groups based on their mothers' late pregnancy cortisol values: high and low prenatal cortisol groups. A trend was found for the high cortisol infants to be delivered earlier than the low cortisol group. Furthermore, the behavioral observations showed the higher prenatal cortisol group to display more crying, fussing, and negative facial expressions. Supporting these findings, maternal reports on temperament also showed these infants to have more difficult behavior: They had higher scores on emotion and activity. The differences between the infants were strongest at the youngest ages (weeks 1–7).

www.ingramcontent.com/pod-product-compliance
Lightning Source LLC
LaVergne TN
LVHW082357200926
848481LV00012B/3595
9781604151237